Pattern

Tricia Guild
Pattern

Special photography by James Merrell
Text by Elspeth Thompson with Tricia Guild

RIZZOLI
NEW YORK

For Lola, Alexander, George and Sebastian, who create beautiful patterns

contents

Work in progress

Living pattern

Patterns can be free or contained, spontaneous or harmonious, fluid or rigid, classical or innovative, inspirational or balanced, colored or neutral, subtle or vivacious. It is this ever-changing spirit of pattern that informs my work as a designer—along with the desire to create and recreate the continuous movement and growth that patterns can breathe into the heart of each textile, giving soul and energy to the spaces in which we live. The position of each leaf, petal, and pencil mark can change the dynamic and flow in an instant. Remove a flower, and the pattern becomes a stripe; add a leaf and suddenly one sees a square; enlarge the scale, and a classic design becomes contemporary. This alchemy is the source of continual inspiration, contemplation, and delight. Color changes bring further transformations: Soften the black or remove it for a subtle shift in character; paint an outline to define an image; add chartreuse, and the pink has a different vitality. Each pattern that is created is the product of such reflections—a constant looking and sensing process, whether in the studio or at a printing table, a weaving loom or a vat of dye—searching for the rhythm that feels right. Like color, pattern has the power to change the look and mood of a room. But it also needs skillful handling to work well, particularly where a mix of patterns and colors is concerned. This book aims to inspire and instruct by illustrating the impact of different patterns in a huge range of interior spaces and experimenting to create a wide variety of styles and moods.

It is hard to pinpoint where inspiration comes from, but it will usually begin with a feeling or observation, born on a trip abroad, perhaps, and developed through the discovery of old document fabrics in an archive book, the colors in a painting, or a piece of old ceramic. There is a gathering of images, swatches, fragments, and photographs to make a collage board, which will provide the seed from which a new collection will grow. The patchwork of painted artwork on the previous pages forms the basis of several new patterns in a variety of colorways that are halfway through work on one of our latest collections. This time it was travel to St. Petersburg that provided the spark of inspiration. Although the pattern is never a direct translation, it may be possible to trace the swirling white curlicues of the painted baroque architecture; the lavish decorations inside the palaces; and the brightly embroidered flowers on a piece of folk costume. For me, it's always a deeply absorbing process, which is also extremely personal. By exploring just some of the many different patterns that have inspired and continue to inspire me, and by experimenting with using them in a variety of classic and unexpected ways, I hope in this book to communicate some of my own deep fascination with pattern and encourage others to develop their own.

Tricia Guild.

Historic pattern

Pattern surrounds us wherever we look: from dappled sunlight shining through leaves onto a lawn or the regular repetition of bricks in a wall to the stripes, spots, checks, and florals with which we choose to adorn our clothes and homes. Sometimes the patterns are simple, such as the alternate colored squares of gingham or the interlocking hexagons that form a traditional patchwork; sometimes they are intricate and ornate—think of the myriad of gold threads on an embroidered sari, the colored swirls of a paisley shawl, or the charming flowers, birds, and leaves on hand-painted Chinese wallpaper. From our most ancient beginnings, it seems to have been innate in human nature to look for pattern in our natural surroundings—to observe the regularity in, for instance, the arrangement of petals on a flower, scales on a fish, or stars in the sky—and to seek to replicate such visual rhythms in our man-made environment.

While prehistoric man was still developing the basic necessities of life, he also began creating the first paintings and objects that show both geometric and pictorial designs arranged with a well-developed sense of order. Sometimes these early patterns seem to have been purely ornamental; at other times, it seems certain that particular shapes, colors, and motifs were loaded with religious and cultural significance—clothes that protected the wearer from demons or a device above a doorway to promote good fortune. Islamic art is particularly rich in geometric pattern, partly because some interpretations prohibit the depiction of any living creature. In some cultures the triangle is seen as a symbol of immortality while the circle is suggestive of the cyclical rhythms of life. Sometimes the meaning of a pattern or motif can change from one time or culture to another: the swastika, originally an Indian good-luck symbol, is a classic, if ill-fated, example.

The term "pattern" can be defined as a design composed of one or more images, shapes, or devices, multiplied and arranged in a regular sequence. A single device—from a simple spot or stripe to a complex cartouche or bouquet of roses—is not a pattern, but a unit that can be used to compose a pattern. This single device is usually called a "motif," and the way in which the motifs regularly recur is the "repeat." Different variations of patterns and repeats evolved for particular purposes: large-scale designs are traditionally more commonly used for decorating and upholstery and will most often have a "directional" repeat that can easily be matched up when joining a roll of wallpaper or length of decorator fabric; while smaller, "allover" patterns are naturally more suited to smaller items such as clothes. (However, as we shall see in the course of this book, such rules and traditions can often be broken to great effect.)

The history of pattern can be traced through the development of the designs themselves. One of the simplest and earliest of all patterns is the stripe—horizontal or vertical lines running parallel to one another. When crossed with another stripe running at right angles, a striped pattern evolves into a check or plaid; and should the angle at which the two lines cross be altered, it forms a diamond—another potent design shape in its own right. A third bisecting line forms the equilateral triangle, which can be arranged and rearranged into an infinity of patterns. The first circle was probably formed by the revolutions of a forklike instrument in the sand, and the joining of dots around the perimeter at regular intervals created the star. More complex geometric designs evolved as more interlocking lines were added, culminating in the intricate geometry of Moorish mosaics or the delicate tracery of a Gothic vaulted ceiling. Representations of the natural world also increased in complexity, from the earliest graphic depictions of birds and animals in pre-Columbian weavings to the heavily stylized roses and lilies that decorated the damasks, brocades, and embroideries that traveled along the Silk Route from the Middle Ages onward, to the brightly colored leaf forms, heavily influenced by abstract art of 1940s and '50s Britain.

Patterns are, obviously, inextricably tied up with the means of their production. A major distinction is that between constructed patterns—those in which the design derives from the manipulation of the different elements in the material itself—and applied or surface patterns. The most commonly found constructed patterns are, of course, those in woven fabric, such as damask and tartan, where the direct manipulations of the warp and weft threads, whether previously dyed, woven, or knotted to create different colors or textures, are what build up the pattern as an integrated part of the material itself. Here the pattern is not always made evident by changes in color; sometimes, as in "self-striped" satin or white damask tablecloths, it is the changes in texture—further enhanced by the effect of light and draping on the material—that form the pattern. Surface patterning includes not only printing and many forms of embroidery but also all resist methods, such as tie-dye, ikat (in which the warp and/or weft threads are bound and part-dyed prior to weaving), and batik (in which the pattern is drawn directly onto the cloth in melted wax and then removed after dyeing).

The development of different production techniques played an important part in the evolution of both types of pattern—in particular, the jump from preindustrial methods, such as hand-painting, weaving, embroidering, and printing using hand-held blocks, to mechanized, mass-produced printing and weaving. The first surface patterns were probably made using hands and then other objects on cloth, paper, or the body itself—fingers and primitive brushes could be used to make flowing, linear patterns, while coating the hand, stick, shell, or stone in pigment and then stamping its imprint gave a different effect. From such elementary beginnings it was not long before handmade stamps were created from clay, wood, or metal and used to repeat various designs, sometimes overprinted with another in a different color to form sophisticated, multicolored patterns. These early techniques produced patterns with intrinsic irregularities—where intervals between motifs were judged by eye, for instance, or two hand-blocked patterns overlapped or did not quite meet—which were largely ironed out with the advent of mechanized printing. Different techniques evolved, from copperplate printing to roller printing, perrotine printing (a mechanized version of the block printing that could print three different colors at once) and various forms of screen printing, and now digitalized printing by computer—each with its own effect on the development of pattern. Printing with steel or copper rollers, for instance, allowed for a fineness of detail that was vital for the production of eighteenth-century toile de Jouy, while screen printing can create a more painterly look, and the latest techniques reproduce photographic effects on cloth and paper.

In woven fabrics, the difference between cloth made by hand-operated and by fully mechanized looms is marked by the uniformity of tension in the threads of the latter and the precise regularity of patterns or color changes. In hand weaving, there was scope for the weaver's individual ideas—and even moods, in the tension of the threads—to affect the progression of the pattern, even if he or she was copying a prescribed design. Once the production process was fully mechanized, such variations did not occur. The increased smoothness of machine-woven fabrics in the eighteenth century is one of the factors (along with the development of wash-fast printers' inks) that made the development of more and more complex patterns possible. But there is no doubt that something was sacrificed to progress—indeed, the irregularities of handmade fabrics and wallpapers are now often regarded as part of their charm and exclusivity, as tangible evidence of the skill and effort involved.

Before the days of mechanized production, pattern tended to be labor-intensive and therefore expensive. Highly patterned clothes and furnishings denoted high status, from the embroidery-encrusted jackets of Ottoman emperors to the heavy crewelwork bed hangings of Elizabeth I; and this is still the case today with haute couture ball gowns, where each of the thousands of beaded flowers is created and sewn on by hand. Changing color technology also had its effect on pattern: earlier designs show the subtle muted shades of natural dyestuffs, but the advent of easily available chemical dyes in the 1800s made possible the brightly colored printed cottons and chintzes that have been common ever since.

Over the centuries, a classifying language has developed among textile designers and others who work with pattern. Patterns are traditionally divided into four main groups, categorized by the type of ornament they employ—geometric, floral, pictorial (or conversational), and ethnic—while the type of repeat is described as "side-by-side," "drop" or "half-drop" (where the motifs are slightly dropped down next to the original placing), "brick" (staggered horizontally), "spot," or "allover." Even the designs themselves are often identified by curious-sounding terms that operate as a shorthand for different styles, among them "neats" (spaced-out layouts of small-scale floral or geometric motifs, usually on a white ground); "ditsies" (sprinkled, spriglike designs); "dobbies" (a small, woven-in geometric ornament); and "dumb-dumbs" (motifs deemed so inoffensive as to make no statement at all). At times the terms for the different fabrics and the designs themselves have become almost interchangeable. Calico, for instance, is a tightly woven cotton cloth (its name taken from the Indian city of Calicut, its port of origin), but for many it has become synonymous with the brightly colored, allover small-scale floral designs with which it was printed and made into *Little House on the Prairie* frocks. Likewise, chintz is, in fact, a glaze-covered cloth of Indian origin; but in many countries it is often associated with the large-scale floral designs used to create the classic "English country house" look.

The most basic pattern types can be found throughout history and all over the world. Stripes are stripes, whether woven in the vibrant contrasting bands of the kente cloths worn by the Ashanti tribes of Ghana; in the subtle gray, blue, and white cottons of Gustavian Sweden; or printed with the dazzling black-and-white lines of op art. Similar zigzag designs crop up in Navajo blankets from pre-Columbian America, the ikat weaves of India and Indonesia, and the subtly graduated bargello upholstery of Renaissance Florence. And remarkable parallels can be drawn between the intricate patterns of ancient Peruvian and Fair Isle knitting. Others are identified with one country of origin, even if latter-day versions have made their way across international boundaries and into the modern-day Western vernacular. Tartan, for instance, will always be associated with Scotland, even though plaid woven fabrics, in which the colors of warp and weft combine to form another color where they cross, are common all over the world. The Greek "key" design, often printed or woven into borders, will always be associated with the Ancient World, even if most existing versions date from eighteenth-century France and England, where the early printing industry coincided with the revival of classical antiquity in the Empire and neoclassical styles. And a certain combination of flowers, stripes, and allover pattern, gaily printed in bright colors, will always be known as "Provençal," no matter what its country of origin.

It is quite common for the history of a pattern to be woven into its very name: moires, ombrés, and toile de Jouy are obviously French, while "indiennes," with their heavily stylized birds, trees, and flowers in Provençal-type colorways, are French interpretations of Indian printed cottons, dating from the ban on importing Indian cottons to France, for trade protection reasons, from 1686 to 1759. Trade routes and regulations had an enormous influence on the development of pattern. The rich exchange between the cities and countries encountered along the Silk Route can clearly be seen in the ornate embroidered brocades and woven damasks that were introduced to Europe from the Middle Ages onward, endlessly interpreted and reinterpreted along the way. Then the introduction of fully mechanized mills in early-nineteenth-century Europe saw anglicized versions of Indian and Persian patterns being produced specifically for the Eastern market—as well as "Manchester Prints" and French cotton printed with "tribal" motifs in classical cartouches destined for colonial Africa.

More recently, public events have provided the inspiration for patterns that ended up as fabric or wallpaper. A Provencal-style print featuring an image of the Eiffel Tower appeared on a cotton fabric produced to commemorate the 1889 Universal Exposition in Paris, while designs incorporating motifs taken from lunar explorations, depictions of molecular structures, and new inventions such as television were commonplace in 1940s and '50s Britain. Modern art movements also found their way into fabric and wallpaper patterns, from the angular architectural forms of French cubism and Russian constructivism to the "form follows function" woven stripes and checks of Bauhaus Germany, the painterly omega designs of the Bloomsbury Group, and the mesmerizing swirls and illusions of 1960s pop and op art. Many artists tried their hand at fabric design, often with stunning results that have stood the test of time. Among the most notable are

Raoul Dufy's stylized figures and landscapes for Bianchini-Ferier in the 1920s, John Piper's reinterpretations of the English countryside for David Whitehead in the 1950s, Marino Marini's Horse and Rider prints for Edinburgh Weavers in 1960, Keith Haring's graffiti prints for Stephen Sprouse in 1980s New York, and Howard Hodgkin's best-selling tulip design for Designers Guild.

Today, there is probably more popular interest in pattern than ever before. The fashion industry is using pattern in more variety and combinations than in the past; and after what seems like decades of white walls, wallpaper is making a timely comeback in our interiors. There has never been such a rich variety of strongly patterned furnishing fabrics available, from sumptuous cut velvets and shimmering silks to colorful plaids and florals, both traditional and modern. It seems a fitting time to celebrate pattern in all of its diversity, and this book aims to do just that, looking at the evolution of the main different pattern groups through history—using both traditional and contemporary examples—and illustrating their use in the modern interior in a variety of original, often surprising and inspired, ways.

Coat of a high-ranking official in 19th-century Bukhara featuring a sumptuous layering of pattern on pattern: gold brocade embroidery on red silk velvet, with silk ikat lining and woven and embroidered border.

The silk route

Samarkand, Bukhara, Damascus, Tashkent, the Taklamakan Desert—just the names of some of the cities and regions on the Silk Route, the world's oldest and best-known trading route, still conjure up an air of faraway exoticism. These days, though still considered a luxury, silk can easily be found on every major shopping street, but there was a time when people would travel seven thousand miles in search of this soft, sheeny fabric, woven from filaments of the cocoons of the silk moth, *Bombyx mori*.

It is thought that the first silk fabrics date back to Shang dynasty China (1500–1050 BC), and for many centuries the Chinese closely guarded the secrets of its production, aware that its great beauty, strength, warmth, and readiness to take dye set it a cut above other fabrics. The Romans apparently first encountered silk during a campaign against the Parthians in 53 BC, but realized that it could not be produced by these relatively unsophisticated people. For many years the Parthians fiercely protected its source, acting as middlemen between the Roman Empire and the mysterious "Seres" or "Silk People" of China.

Myths abound as to how the secrets of silk weaving were finally wrested from China and transported to the West. One story relates that a Chinese princess, destined for marriage to the king of neighboring Khotan but desperate to ensure a supply of silk for her own gowns, secreted the cocoons of a few silkworms in her elaborate headdress; other legends tell how, in the sixth century AD, two monks smuggled some cocoons to Byzantium in hollowed-out walking sticks. Early attempts at sericulture in the West failed dismally. Silk worms are delicate creatures, sensitive to noise and drafts, who feed only on the leaves of the rare white mulberry, *Morus alba*. The efforts of King James I of England to establish silk production in his country were famously thwarted when it was discovered that he had ordered the planting of ten thousand of the wrong type of tree.

It was in around the second century BC that the first caravans set out from China in active search of the West, laden with gold, ivory, precious stones, and glass, as well as silk, and returning with furs, ceramics, spices, lacquer, and iron from the Middle East and the Mediterranean. The first European to penetrate all the way by land to the unknown vastness of China was Marco Polo, who left Venice in 1271, aged just seventeen, and documented his travels across Persia and central Asia to the court of Kublai Khan at the

site of present-day Beijing and to his summer palace at Xanadu. From then on until its demise two hundred years later, this long and winding route, or rather series of routes, was populated by a two-way traffic of caravans carrying not just silk from China but spices and precious stones from India, silver from Persia, ornate woven and embroidered textiles from Byzantium, Asian ceramics, rare plants, medicines, and other coveted commodities. The overland roads wound around northwest China, circumvented the Taklamakan Desert, halted at long-fabled cities such as Bukhara and Samarkand, crossed central Asia, and headed for the Caspian Sea and the eastern Mediterranean, taking in sandstorms, avalanches, banditry, and exorbitant tariffs on the way.

It is hard for us, from a twenty-first-century perspective, to understand fully the extraordinary importance that silk textiles, intricately woven and embroidered with exotic patterns, had at this time. They not only clothed and decorated; they also defined imperial, court, and clerical rank and were always among the offerings bestowed on and received from diplomatic embassies. As highly valuable commercial goods, silk fabrics were transported across long distances, with customs duties or tributes frequently paid in silk and gold-embroidered textiles. Photographs rarely do justice to the skill and labor involved. Take the time to visit a museum such as the Victoria & Albert in London, where fine collections of old silk textiles are held, and take a close look at the ornate brocade coats of the Ottoman sultans or the richly patterned *suzani* bridal awnings of Uzbekistan. Better still, travel to the Silk Route countries themselves to see how the old skills are surviving, in spite of centuries of war and political upheaval and increasing commercialization.

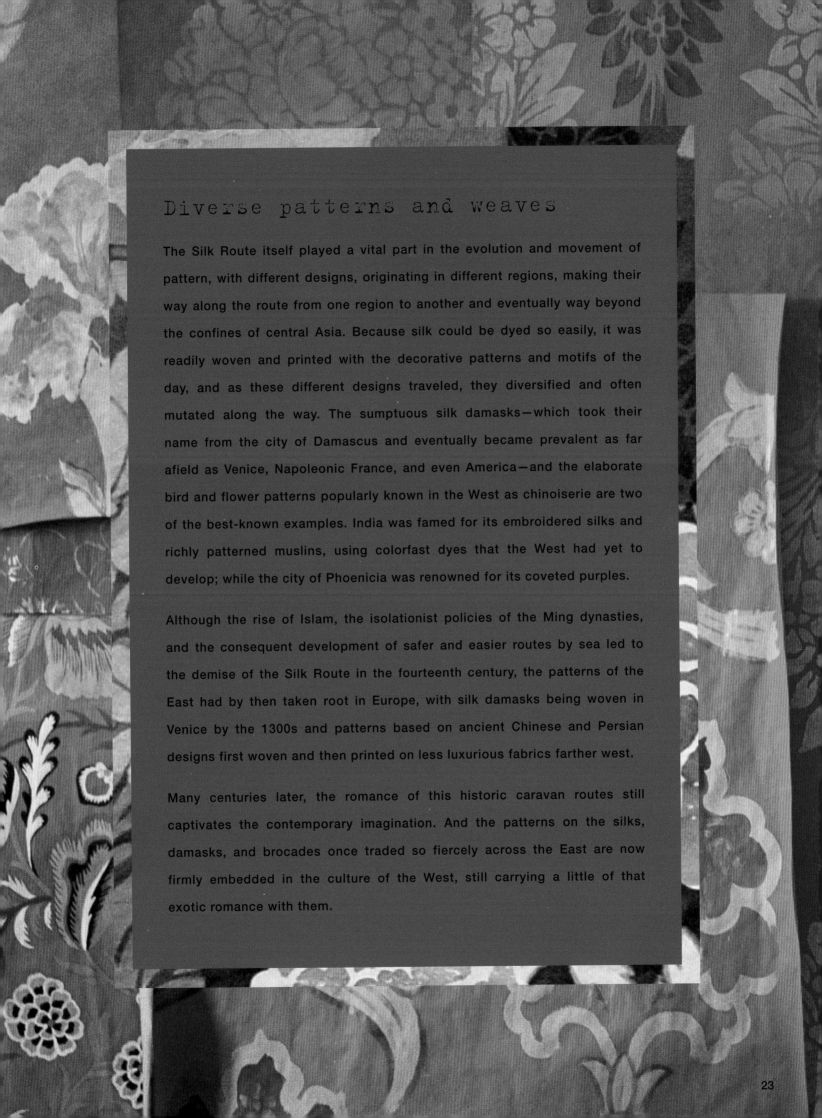

Diverse patterns and weaves

The Silk Route itself played a vital part in the evolution and movement of pattern, with different designs, originating in different regions, making their way along the route from one region to another and eventually way beyond the confines of central Asia. Because silk could be dyed so easily, it was readily woven and printed with the decorative patterns and motifs of the day, and as these different designs traveled, they diversified and often mutated along the way. The sumptuous silk damasks—which took their name from the city of Damascus and eventually became prevalent as far afield as Venice, Napoleonic France, and even America—and the elaborate bird and flower patterns popularly known in the West as chinoiserie are two of the best-known examples. India was famed for its embroidered silks and richly patterned muslins, using colorfast dyes that the West had yet to develop; while the city of Phoenicia was renowned for its coveted purples.

Although the rise of Islam, the isolationist policies of the Ming dynasties, and the consequent development of safer and easier routes by sea led to the demise of the Silk Route in the fourteenth century, the patterns of the East had by then taken root in Europe, with silk damasks being woven in Venice by the 1300s and patterns based on ancient Chinese and Persian designs first woven and then printed on less luxurious fabrics farther west.

Many centuries later, the romance of this historic caravan routes still captivates the contemporary imagination. And the patterns on the silks, damasks, and brocades once traded so fiercely across the East are now firmly embedded in the culture of the West, still carrying a little of that exotic romance with them.

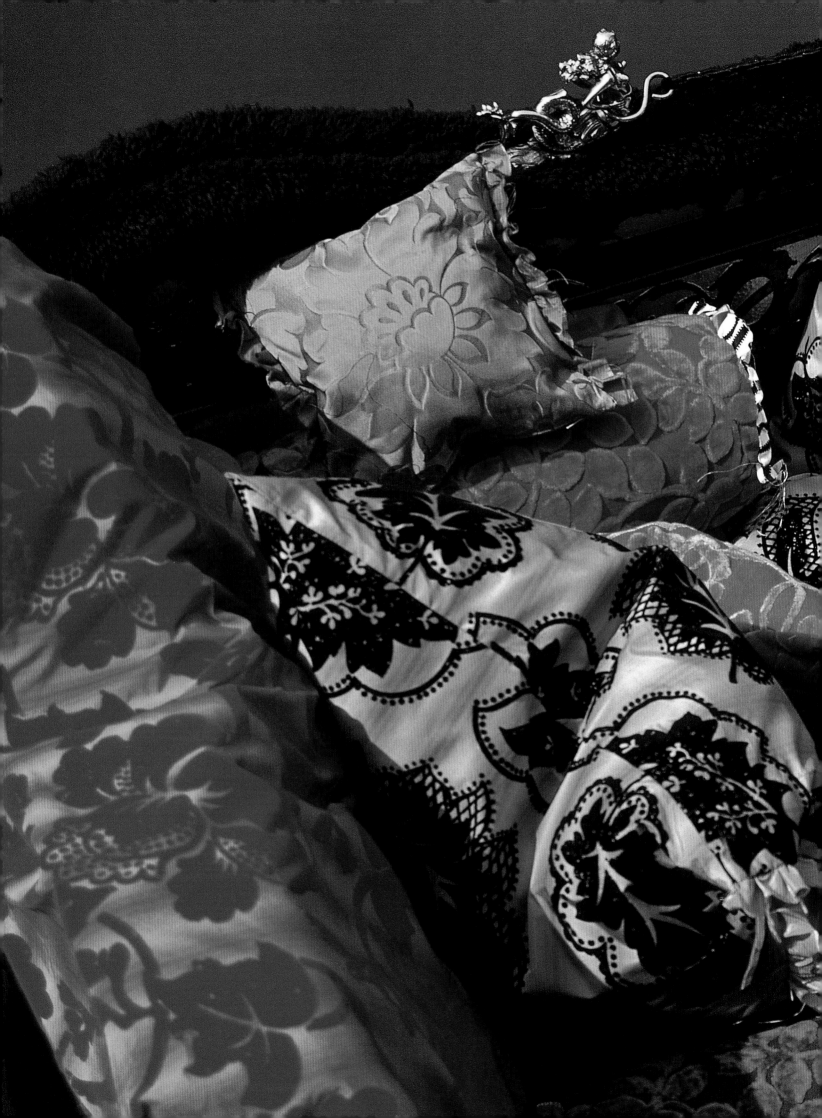

Venetian opulence

Whether printed, woven, or embroidered, pattern on fabric or paper has traditionally been achieved by varying degrees of additional labor. Think of the elaborate scrolling patterns of Jacobean crewelwork; the intricate jacquard weaves of French Huguenot ribbons; the hand-stitched beads and sequins on an haute couture gown. This is why, over the centuries, pattern has tended to be associated with wealth, and an excess of pattern with decadence. Partly as a response to the evermore complicated patterns of the art nouveau movement, the Austrian architect Adolf Loos made his infamous pronouncement "All ornament is crime." To this day, an obvious way to create an atmosphere of opulence and wealth is to employ layer upon layer of luxurious pattern. When orchestrating other moods in an interior—one of freshness or exuberance, for example—a designer must make room for plain areas and simple, uncomplicated patterns. But if opulence is the effect required, such restraint can be forgotten.

Venetian palaces are among the most opulently decorated buildings in Europe, and this seventeenth-century palazzo is no exception. From the ornate, painted, paneled ceiling and gilded cornices to frescoed walls, faux marble architraves, and terrazzo stone floors, every inch of the original architecture was already covered in pattern. One response might have been to tone down the furnishings, to upholster the existing gilded and inlaid furniture with plain beige linens or discreet stripes and plaids. But because the floor and wall patterns, though ornate, are mainly in neutral colors, it was possible to transform the somewhat heavy atmosphere of the place with exuberant color and pattern. Opulent silks and damasks are a fitting choice, as it was from Venice that Marco Polo set forth along the old Silk Route to China in the thirteenth century. The jewel-bright silk damasks, cut velvets, and striped and flock fabrics that have been used through all the rooms marry all the opulence of old Venice with a bold contemporary elegance that is totally twenty-first century.

Here, in the entrance hall, an exuberant mix of flock damasks, stripes, and leaf designs in orange, pink, and fuchsia silks sets the scene for what is to follow. The existing architecture is respected. The subtle tones and swirling shapes of the terrazzo floor and figurative wall fresco are perfectly complemented by the ornate damask and cut silk patterns, with the orange silk shades echoing the golden wooden wall paneling. These warm, joyful colors, further enlivened by the daring juxtaposition of various different stripes with floral flock velvets on the inlaid cherry-wood sofa and carved wooden chairs, banish any air of historical heaviness and make this grand, imposing space feel welcoming and lived-in. The candy-stripe swirls of Venetian Murano glass add another fitting layer of pattern.

Flock printing

Flock wallpapers are now more common than flocked fabric, but flock powdered wool, a waste product from the woolen cloth industry, was first applied to cloth. Early patterns were simple linear designs dating from the early seventeenth century; it was not until the 1730s that the familiar imitations of damask and cut velvet patterns began to appear. The first flock wallpapers were invented to imitate cut velvet wall hangings. They proved not only cheaper but also harder wearing—the turpentine used for fixing the flock also repelled moths. Some of the large-scale formal designs have been in production ever since. Modern versions use rayon flock applied with a flock gun, but almost entirely for historical renovation projects.

The time is ripe for a revival, using contemporary patterns and colors.

Painted frescoes

As one of the largest surface areas in a room, and uninterrupted by furniture, furnishings, and itinerant feet, ceilings presented an unrivaled opportunity for decoration until fashions changed fairly recently. Here in this seventeenth-century Venetian palazzo, the decorative borders, Greek key designs, and putti astride dolphins have been executed in a light style and subtle color palette, which complement, rather than overpowering the ornate glass chandelier.

Silk damask

"Damasked" silks and velvets were probably introduced to Venice by Persian exiles in the fourteenth century, but the Venetians developed designs that were all their own—their shimmering patterns, often depicted on a gold ground, were inspired, perhaps, by the magnificent mosaics of Basilica di San Marco, or the quivering reflections of the buildings in the water outside. Damask was originally a very prestigious fabric, favored by the rich, and its lustrous finish, coupled with restrained formal designs, is still used to give a grand impression. Over the years, though, it has become synonymous with an almost institutionalized form of luxury, so it is high time to give the fabric a fresh, modern look.

The large-scale design used here is just what is needed in the light, airy bedroom of this same Venetian palazzo. The room's natural grandeur is enhanced by an assured and sophisticated mix of patterns. The modern damask that hangs at the windows and also covers one of the walls is the perfect complement to the big, blowsy peony print with its gold, mossy ground. In fact, this beautiful design incorporates three different layers of pattern: the bright painterly flowers are printed onto a damask fabric, itself woven with textured flower shapes and printed with a graphic stencil design of scrolling flowers and leaves. This lavish layering of pattern upon pattern within the same fabric brings an extraordinary depth to the design and makes the painterly style of the flowers stand out all the more. Alternating this fabric with the subtle gold silk damask and an ombré striped silk for the curtains ensures that the flowers are appreciated in all their abundant glory.

Blue velvet

The frescoed ceiling, terrazzo floor, and spectacular glass chandelier set the tone of richly patterned opulence in this second-floor salon, and it was hard to resist adding more. Layer upon layer of silk stripes, damasks, and cut velvets, at the windows, on the furniture, and even covering the walls, create a cocoon of luxury and warmth. The woven silk damask on the walls is particularly luxurious and harks back to a time when fabrics were used quite literally to keep in the warmth in large, cold rooms. The practice is still relatively common in parts of Europe, with the fabric stretched across wooden strips attached to the walls. This can be emulated more simply by hanging large banners of fabric. Here, the gorgeous swirling pattern has been woven on an ombré-shaded ground—a specialized technique involving the warp threads being set up by hand in subtly graduating stripes—which further contributes to the feeling of richness; but the colors, a vibrant turquoise and gold-tinged mossy green, are fresh and modern.

Turquoise serves as the link with the many other patterns in the room—the bold modern take on damask in flock on linen at the window, the striped ombré silk used for one drapery and the soft valance, and the cut velvet floral and leaf designs on the low modern chairs. The high ceilings and tall windows enable large-scale pattern to be used to bold effect as draperies; but using an asymmetrical arrangement with a strong self-stripe on one side is a slightly eccentric touch that brings us back firmly to the twenty-first century and banishes any feeling of stuffiness that might be associated with traditional damask-based patterns. Other subtle color links enable the other different patterns to mix harmoniously. The cut velvet designs on the chairs—one a leaf and one a stylized flower—share the same dark charcoal background, while just a glimpse of fuchsia pink in a striped silk drapery lining and on the back of one of the cushions picks up on the view through the open doorway. Plenty of glass and mirrors catch the glittering light reflected from the water outside.

Damask

The name describes a woven fabric in which the pattern—usually a large-scale formal design featuring highly stylized floral motifs—is formed by the contrast of shiny warp-face areas and matte weft-face areas and the way in which the light falls on them. Named after the city of Damascus, the fabric was first encountered by Marco Polo on the Silk Route and introduced to Europe on his return to Venice in 1295. Depending on the colors used, damask cloth can be self-patterned or two-toned, and the pattern is reversible. Although noted for its lustrous finish, it is remarkably hard-wearing. Woven silk damasks continued to be the inspiration for wallpaper designs of the wealthy for many centuries, while cheaper printed versions soon sprang up for the mass market.

Bringing pattern into modern spaces gives them such spontaneity.

White is wonderful, but there are other, more exciting options.

Contemporary cut velvet

Flock wallpaper and cut velvet are two types of pattern that have become stuck in the past. Associated with grand Victorian drawing rooms and Indian restaurants, flock would not seem the obvious choice for this minimal contemporary interior, while cut velvet is more likely to be found on scarves and evening dresses than upholstering a streamlined modern sofa. Yet pattern is nothing if not flexible, and the challenge of finding new ways to reinvent old influences for the twenty-first century proved irresistible in this modernist living room. With its plain white walls, pale stone floors, and light pouring in through huge glass windows, the room was a blank canvas. Painting one wall bright pink would have been a bold move, following the example of the Mexican architect Luis Barragán. Using pattern plus texture in the form of flock wallpaper takes the concept several steps further and is totally unexpected. Uninterrupted by pictures, mirrors, or other conventional trappings, the pattern becomes the main statement in the room—the repeated motifs as mesmerizing as the echoing images in an Andy Warhol screen print. The end result is a splendid screen against which the curvy red and white furniture and spindly spires of foxgloves stand out in sculptural relief. Instead of draperies, banners of fabric can be slid along runners to filter the sun as required. One is the same flock pattern as the wall but printed on pink linen; the other is a striped silk whose jewel-bright colors are further illuminated by the light shining through them. This simple treatment of fabric allows the patterns to be seen to full effect: the bunching and pleating commonly involved in curtain-making means the design often ends up buried in the folds.

Instead of contrasting solid-colored fabric for the upholstery, a cut velvet in a similar shade but a different pattern was used, adding another layer of soft, luxurious texture in this potentially stark setting. (Incidentally, this is the same pattern, but in another color, as the cut velvet used for the sofas in the Venetian palazzo on pages 28–37—further proof of the adaptability of pattern as part of two totally different looks.) Not a texture usually associated with modernist furniture, cut velvet has also been used for cushions on the sofa and to upholster the chrome-legged footstool and Eero Saarinen tulip chairs. In the face of all this swirling pink pattern, some contrast was definitely needed, and the heavy linen tweed is perfect, adding a note of coolness but with an organic texture, flecked with myriad of different threads, which can more than hold its own among the luxurious flocks and velvets. The turquoise is picked up in the form of accents: the flock-printed cushions and the flowers on the graphic red rug—a strong contemporary pattern with strands of stylized blossoms falling across it. A single splash of emerald green in the ruffled silk damask cushion is a reminder of the natural landscape beyond, drawing the eye upward to the strip of window, which works like a stripe of green at the top of the patterned pink wall.

A black and white palette with pink accents, shiny black textures, and

fragile white blossom breathe an air of the Far East into this room.

Cloisonné

The fabrics and patterns of the Silk Route spread East as well as West. This glamorous black-and-white scheme was loosely inspired by the mixture of patterns on a twentieth-century silk kimono. The subtly Asian feel, underscored by details such as the fragile white blossoms on the fabric on the chair and the shiny lacquer-look lamp, is accentuated by the classic Far Eastern color scheme: black and white with small splashes of pink and bright red.

A restricted color scheme is always liberating when it comes to using pattern, making possible the juxtaposition of three different floral-based patterns on the paneled walls: a damask-inspired print above the fireplace, a stenciled flower pattern on either side, and the large graphic blooms beneath the chair rail. The effect of the last is akin to a wide floral border running around the base of the walls, anchoring the other designs in place. It is picked up again in the draperies, which have a slightly more complicated design incorporating an ornate ecru butterfly. This large pattern was inspired partly by the cloisonné technique for decorating with enamel. The large areas of slightly raised and glossy color call to mind the brilliant pools of shiny enamel on Eastern metal plates and jugs.

Black-and-white rooms cannot help but also have retro associations. There are shades of pop and op art in the dazzling mix of patterns and a nod to the hound's-tooth checked suits of London's Carnaby Street in the 1960s.

Jewel box

Patterns inspired by the Silk Route have been used for yet another transformation of the living room in my London home. The tall room has been stripped to a bare elegant minimum—the perfect backdrop for using these bold, formal fabrics in a modern, unstructured way. The dividing doors have been painted a brilliant Indian turquoise, and the walls a softer, paler shade of blue, against which the jewel-bright colors of flock silks and damasks can sing out in style.

One set of windows is dressed with a bold damask design in bright pink flock on white silk, over a striped turquoise silk with a contrasting strip of mauve. At the other end of the room, the same damask design in black-and-white flock silk is joined by another silk flock pattern in rich magenta on pink, with a contrasting under-drapery of turquoise and lime green. The draperies are neither lined nor pleated, in order to give these once rather formal patterns a fresh, relaxed feel and to let the sunlight illuminate the colors and swirling shapes of the design. The patterns and colors complement one another and provide subtle links between the different patterns and elements in the room: the same damask pattern in two contrasting colors; the same bright pinks in two different patterns; the contrasting colors, which pick up the turquoise paint, the mauve upholstery, the green glass tables by MDF Italia. The black-and-white print works particularly well alongside the modern furniture.

kimono

Kimono patterns

The patterns for informal kimonos were created by the *shiboru* process (Japanese tie-dye), or by paste-resist methods resembling batik, while many of the more formal robes had allover patterns that were painted freehand. Motifs came mainly from the natural world and were chosen for their symbolic meaning, as well as their beauty: clouds, cranes, and chrysanthemums for good fortune, long life, and happiness; bamboo for fortitude and hard work; paired ducks for harmony in marriage; and peonies for well-being and prosperity.

Costumes decorated with plum and peach blossom were worn for special occasions, and seasonal flower motifs were favored for the popular spring and late-summer cherry blossom and chrysanthemum festivals.

Asian

The patterns and colors of Japanese kimonos provide inspiration for a subtle mixture of colors and patterns in modern-day interiors. Peony and blossom prints are often suggestive of the East, especially in these unusual color palettes. The flower and butterfly pattern on this page, in a contrasting colorway of grape, cyclamen pink, and chartreuse, has echoes of Japanese cherry blossom—the national flower of Japan, celebrated in paintings and fabric designs, as well as elaborate outdoor festivals each spring. When used in black and white, as shown on pages 43–45 it created an air of drama and glamour; here the effect is softer, the subtle Eastern feel accentuated by the low modern furniture, cushions on the floor, and minimalist flower arrangements. The dominant patterns in the room are flowers and stripes, all linked by a subtle use of color. Exactly the same colors of the large floral print are picked up in the cut velvet stripes on the low modern sofa and chairs, with a chartreuse print on the walls (with lime green panel below) and a bright pink peony print and ombré stripe at the windows.

Camellias and peonies are popular in fabric designs in both the East and the West—not least because that moment of peak perfection, when those gorgeous ephemeral petals are about to burst, can be captured forever. Used here on draperies, their breathtaking beauty brings an awareness of the fragility of the natural world into interiors of any style. Simple arrangements of real flowers—bright peonies and Icelandic poppies—are the perfect complement.

East to Japan

The patterns and techniques of Chinese silk making also penetrated east to Japan, where a lively silk industry sprang up around the creation of traditional kimonos. These highly decorative and ritualistic garments—standard in shape and employing large expanses of contrasting fabric—offered a superb "blank canvas" for different patterns. Their heyday was the Heian period (794–1185 AD), when up to twelve unlined kimonos might be worn at once, with layers of pattern and color visible at the sleeve edges and collar; members of the court might wear up to sixteen different layers.

Over the centuries, the kimono has risen and fallen in popularity many times, but there are still many stunning new and vintage garments to be found. Though the basic shape has remained the same, with the color of the wide *obi* sash changing according to the age and status of the wearer, it is easy to see the influence of European and American fashions in the fabric and patterns, and that of avant-garde Japanese designers who are adapting traditional techniques in innovative ways. Most modern Japanese women possess only one kimono, for their coming-of-age celebrations at the age of nineteen, and the elaborate costumes worn for weddings tend to be rented. Only in small rural towns and on tiny islands is one likely to come across women wearing the kimono as everyday dress.

Botanical paintings of tree peonies and a lotus flower from eighteenth- and nineteenth-century collections of botanical art, showing the graphic attention to detail common in such illustrations.

56

Botanical

As some of the most exquisite and ephemeral products of the natural world, flowers are an obvious choice as motifs for textile and wallpaper patterns. By surrounding ourselves with their images, we bring some of the beauty of the natural world inside, where it can be appreciated whatever the season or time of day, or however far-flung the provenance of the plant in question. There are flowery patterns to suit every mood and style: simple girlish buds and sprigs on calico, lustrous damasks and heavily embroidered brocades featuring lotus flowers and stylized *fleurs-de-lis*, cozy cabbage rose chintzes, and funky modern and retro prints.

Flowers, leaves, and trees feature in some of the earliest patterned fabrics, such as the richly decorated *tapa* bark cloths from Polynesia, still made by hand in the Pacific islands, and the *palmatae* or ceremonial robes embroidered with golden palms worn by successful generals on their triumphal entry into ancient Rome. Sometimes the flowers were overlaid with symbolism long since lost to us. White lilies signified the purity of the Virgin to medieval Christians; while the red rose is an ancient symbol of divine love for many cultures; and the tulip, as the first flower to bloom on the central Asian steppes after rain, was a symbol of fertility for the embroiderers of suzani bridal cloths in Uzbekistan. From earliest history to the present day, flowers have never gone out of fashion in clothing or interior decoration: think of the brightly colored chrysanthemums on Japanese obi or sashes, the "hearts and flowers" patchworks of colonial North America, and the honeysuckle, tulips, and checker lillies of William Morris's three best-selling designs—not to mention Liberty-print lawns, Laura Ashley's rosebuds, and the recent revival of countrified, vintage-look florals. It is ironic that the mass-production techniques that have made printed flower fabric so popular were also the cause of so many people leaving the countryside to work in the towns. From the Industrial Revolution onward, following the march of progress all over the world, the flowers on people's walls and clothes are often, on one level, a poignant reminder of the natural surroundings they have lost.

Long before the advent of photography, drawings, etchings, and paintings were the only method of capturing ephemeral flowers and plants permanently on paper; and these, in turn, had an influence on fabric and furnishing designs. *Gerard's Herball* of 1597 was the first botanical book produced in England, and its graphic woodcuts prove surprisingly accurate to this day. Books of elaborate flower illustrations, called florilegia, such as those of Carolus Clusius (1605) and Emanuel Sweert (1612), soon followed. Many embroiderers, and later textile designers, such as William Morris, took inspiration directly from their pages, or from pattern books closely based on botanical drawings. Later, the exquisite rose prints of Pierre-Joseph Redouté (1759–1840), employed by the Empress Josephine to record the rare plants in her garden, provided inspiration for glorious flowered cottons and chintzes, while studies such as those by Priscilla Susan Bury's of hippeastrums, crinums, and amaryllis from nineteenth-century Mexico continue to inspire modern designers.

Plant hunters and artists

The history of botanical depiction in Europe is bound up with the progress of foreign exploration. Before about 1560, most plants grown in European gardens were native ones; but from the mid-sixteenth century onward, species from all around the world flooded into Europe: tulips, hyacinths and lilies from Turkey; tradescantias, evening primrose, Virginia creeper, and Michaelmas daisies from America; succulents, pelargoniums, crinum lilies, and amaryllis from the Dutch colony at the Cape of Good Hope; rhododendrons from India; fuchsias and dahlias from Mexico; peonies, roses, chrysanthemums, and camellias from China; and irises and maples from Japan. Botanists were often sent on trader and explorer ships, along with artists to record their discoveries; until the invention of the Wardian case (a kind of miniature portable greenhouse) in the 1830s, transporting the plants themselves across stormy seas, often to a complete change of climate, proved an erratic and risky business. Botanical artists were also employed by nurserymen to spread the news about the plants and bulbs they had for sale: many of the famous Dutch flower paintings of the seventeenth century were, in fact, glorified advertisements for tulip bulbs. The minute accuracy required to portray the plants in all their detail, coupled with a necessity to illustrate all their botanical parts, often gave such drawings a distinctive, stylized charm all their own. The style still provides inspiration for artists and fabric designers today, as can be seen from the bold pink peony print used in the paneled room on the following pages and the monochrome zinnia on page 73, as closely observed as a botanical engraving.

Often, though, the images are not faithful depictions of the original—indeed, the heavy stylization of the plants and flowers can be vital to the design's appeal. Sometimes this was not entirely intentional: Jacobean crewelwork shows recently discovered flowers such as tulips and irises, so exotic that they were not even to be found in the latest florilegia, transformed into "trees" with serpentine trunks and curiously outlandish blooms. And as silks and damasks traveled along the Silk Route, the peonies, moss roses, and lilies native to China mutated into graphic, heavily stylized forms, while the prints and chintzes made in India for export to Europe often took considerable liberties with the images of English garden flowers they were asked to emulate. At other times, of course, the graphic stylization of the flowers is an intentional and integral part of the pattern—from the generic allover prints on Liberty lawn to graphic 1960s poppy prints by the Finnish firm Marimekko and the floral designs that launched Designers Guild back in the 1970s. Flowers are still at the heart of Designers Guild designs, with inspiration coming from real garden flowers, old document prints, and the graphic designs of pop and op art (the striking black-and-white design used to such stunning effect on pages 82–85).

The large peony print is the star in this paneled room, with

the subtler ombré stripes and cut velvet patterns paying homage.

Flowers in print

The large stylized peony print used in the paneled room on the preceding pages is a modern reinterpretation of the style of old botanical prints. The size of the flower is unexpected (though totally in keeping with the scale of the architecture); this surprise brings a joyful sense of exuberance to the restrained classical proportions of the space. Equally unconventional is the asymmetrical use of patterned fabrics at the window—the peony print in red this time and a striking silk stripe in shades of persimmon, pink, and blue. This juxtaposition of florals, stripes, and cut velvets works because of the bold color links and dramatic sense of scale.

Historically, wallpaper has often been used to pick out the paneling on walls, but the scale and modernity of this print give it more of the impact of a contemporary painting or screen print. Using a strong color in between and beneath the chair rail—a rich fuchsia in a stencil-block print in a damask effect—seems to anchor the design in the room, preventing the large-scale pattern from becoming overpowering. At the window, the linen draperies show the same flowers in a slightly more complicated design—the fabric is printed with a half-drop and uses many different images of the flower motif, whereas the wallpaper has just two. Alternating the floral draperies with an elegant ombré-striped silk in the same scarlet and pink and a contrasting turquoise blue also helps to balance the impact of the large floral print, and mixing stripes with flowers introduces a slightly tailored feel.

An organic leaf design in cut velvet on the low modern sofa introduces a new pattern and texture. Cut velvet—where the design stands out in raised silk threads against the background fabric—is a traditional technique that is many centuries old; but the effect here, in a stunning deep fuchsia against granite gray-brown linen, is one of thoroughly modern luxury. This is a good illustration of how texture can be used to add new layers of pattern without their competing: the neutral ground enables the pattern to be instantly visible and attractive, while still allowing the sofa to read as solid pink (as do the stencil-printed dado panels).

The other secret of mixing pattern is to keep the key tones the same. Red, pink, and turquoise are bright colors that occupy the same tonal range; the few slashes of turquoise at the windows, in the cushions, and in the corner lamp are carefully orchestrated. Limiting the number of patterns is important, too: one turquoise cushion on the sofa is in the same cut velvet as the sofa itself, while those on the floor are in a flock silk, which echoes the damask design on the walls. In this way, a liaison is formed between the different patterns in the room that links them subtly together while in no way detracting from their seemingly spontaneous charm.

Cherry blossom and magnolia

Flowers of the East are a suitably sybaritic choice for bedrooms, and the cherry blossom and magnolia prints used in this French country bedroom are singularly seductive. Choosing two different patterns brings charm and originality where one might have been merely pretty— a bold move, but the fact they are both printed on damask, in a similar color scheme and with the same striped braid border, allows them to work well together.

Each of the flower patterns brings something different to the room's mood. The cherry blossom design is very fragile, with the flowers loosely painted in watery colors and the white of the original cloth showing through, while the magnolia has stronger, fleshier blooms, which look grand and voluptuous by comparison. The simple, loose gathering at the top of the draperies allows these beautiful patterns to be seen in full, while the striped edging gives the feminine fabrics a slightly tailored feel that is perfectly in keeping with the unaffected formality of the painted, paneled room.

The pale blue damask ground has another flower design woven into it, adding another layer of texture and pattern, but it is the pinks and rich berry tones that provide the stepping-off point for the other unifying elements— striped silk cushions on the bed, the gold-flecked voile curtains that mark the way to the bathroom, and, of course, the braid on the curtains. Note the simpler version of the magnolia print used as a wallpaper, each bloom standing out in all its blushing beauty. And of course, the room would not be complete without plenty of real, fresh flowers—garden roses and anemones in the same palette of pink-tinged whites and creams.

Garden flowers

Bouquets are popular with designers, as they offer an attractive and natural way of combining a number of different flowers in a single motif. Loose bunches of flowers, rather than elaborate nosegays or single graphic blooms, tend to give the designs an informal country feeling; and with their associations of romance, gift giving, and abundance, such patterns are popular in bedrooms and living and dining rooms. Because these are, more often than not, large and quite complex patterns, they are usually not mixed with many others—coordinating neutrals and plenty of fresh flowers provide the perfect complement.

In this French country living room, large bunches of roses, peonies, and lupines on crisp white linen bring the clear pinks, blues, and mauves of a traditional perennial border right inside the house. This exuberant pattern is allowed to sing out in style, so the other furnishings have been left intentionally simple, with lots of white, a few discreet stripes and plaids in coordinating colors, and a careful use of just a few other floral designs. White-painted walls, white linen on the sofa, and white muslin voile at the windows (some with a woven pink stripe) create a cool, neutral backdrop, while the furniture is also white, from the modern lacquered table and chrome upholstered footstool to the antique carved wooden side tables and chairs.

Such restraint allows for fun elsewhere: a collection of old French farmhouse chairs, washed with white paint, has been upholstered in a witty mix of patterns, including a textured slub silk plaid, a large-scale poppy print, and a flock silk floral, which echoes the cushion on the sofa, using mismatching patterns for seats and backs. Keeping these patterns to just three or four, often alternated with a solid pink linen, keeps the rhythm going and prevents the different elements from appearing disparate. And the room would not be complete without plenty of fresh garden flowers in simple white pitchers and glass vases.

With its abundance of flowers and air of unstudied elegance, this room is a modern-day take on the English country house look, which reached its peak in the early decades of the twentieth century, spreading to America and beyond. What brings it firmly into the twenty-first century is the fresh vibrant color scheme, the unfussy furnishings—not a frill or furbelow in sight—and idiosyncratic touches, such as the mismatched chair coverings and cleverly trimmed cushions. Even the flower arrangements are modern—just one type of flower, mauve delphiniums, pink anemones, or amethyst purple hyacinths, in each vase—to complement, rather than compete with, the flower fabric at the windows.

Etched elegance

This tall, airy living room is an exercise in mixing monochrome patterns. The huge zinnias, printed in faded charcoal and white, might have come straight from a modern-day florilegium—their petals, stamens, and anthers as closely observed as any botanical study and etched like an engraving on heavy cotton satin. No pretty-pretty flowers these; they set the tone for the masculine, tailored use of pattern in this formal part-paneled room.

Neutral tones dominate, from the dynamic peat, gray, and white stripe on the armchair and scatter cushions to the textured chenille tweeds and linens on the sofa and chairs. The black-and-white geometric tiled floor is balanced by a bold use of black-and-white pattern in the striped cushions, black plastic chairs, and circular black tufted rug. The dramatic drop for the draperies enables this large pattern to be displayed to its best advantage, and making them bannerlike, rather than tightly pleated or gathered in the old-fashioned way, prevents the flowers from disappearing into the folds.

Without the flower print, this room could possibly be seen as somewhat over-masculine and soulless; yet blowsy roses or peonies would look out of place alongside all the other graphic patterns. This subtly stylized print provides the perfect balance—pushing the boundaries of the neutral palette while never becoming boring. A large chandelier adds a note of theatrical grandeur. Mixing florals and geometrics has never looked so effortlessly stylish.

73

Timeless Tulips

More than almost any other flower except the rose, the tulip has been an inspiration for artists throughout the centuries. From medieval times, the striking blooms are featured not only in the florilegia from which pattern designers took their inspiration, but also in countless ceramic dishes and tiles for domestic use in the Middle East, the borders and backgrounds of Mogul miniatures, and all manner of paintings. We are all familiar with the seventeenth-century Dutch artists' love affair with the tulip, but many others—as diverse as Breughel, William Morris, and Bloomsbury's Dora Carrington and Howard Hodgkin—have also painted tulips. Perhaps their appeal lies in the fact that tulips themselves look almost as if they have been painted—their petals as glossy as glistening wet paint, streaked and striped as with an artist's brush. They can be found in a dazzling array of colors, shapes, and sizes, from the tiny pointed petals of wild species, such as creamy white *Tulipa turkestanica* to the glamorous lily-flowered 'Marilyn,' fist-sized scarlet blooms of soldier-straight 'General Eisenhower,' and fabulously frilled and feathered parrot varieties. They are stunning in all stages of their growth—tight minaret-shaped buds swelling into splendid sculptural blooms that are held on straight stems at the start, but when cut and brought inside, begin to curve and sway with wayward abandon as the flowers become fully open. They even die beautifully, their petals exploding in a harlequin pile around the vase. Small wonder that they are northern Europe's favorite cut flower.

Tulips are a perennial favorite with fabric designers, whether small, simple blooms in childlike primaries or the most colorful and complex flowers the breeders and bulb merchants have to offer. The striped florists' tulips featured in this living room have a certain formality about them that complements the sumptuous flock damasks and velvets used for the upholstery. These graphic specimens, in darkest purple and crimson streaked with white, are easily beautiful enough to hold their heads among the finest striped silks.

Florals, stripes, and damask designs are used harmoniously together here, the three strong patterns mixing harmoniously because the same palette—fuchsia, pink, taupe, and pearly white—has been used throughout. The stripes on the tulips blend seamlessly with the thick, shiny stripes on the velvet-and-linen-covered sofa, while the flock-printed silk damask at the windows is echoed in similar designs on the cushions and white-on-natural flock chair. This confident use of pattern in a rich but restricted range of colors—no contrasting accents in lime or turquoise here—gives the room a formal air that is in keeping with the architecture. Large expanses of neutrals—bare plaster on the walls, terra-cotta floor tiles, and natural linen grounds for the more ornate fabrics—provide a welcome breathing space.

Old roses modern chintz

Pastel pink walls and a rose-printed chintz sound like the trappings of a traditional English country bedroom, but this modern take on chintz has a fresh and almost funky appeal. The flowers are painterly and dynamic, with a lightness of touch that gives them a look more in common with an impressionist painting than a careful botanical study. And the way in which they are used—combined with strong graphic stripes and plaids in black, white, and scarlet—only adds to the fresh modern feel.

Simple touches such as the edging of a cushion in black-and-white striped silk, and hanging a black, red, and white striped linen banner at the window, counteract the traditional prettiness still associated with roses and chintz. And using a mix of modern fabrics—stripes, solids, and other large-scale florals in the same range of colors—to upholster the pretty painted period chairs brings a certain spontaneous and youthful charm.

Plain painted walls and a large expanse of white on the bed are part of the thoughtful (though apparently careless) balancing act that holds the scheme together. A mixture of florals, plaids, and stripes requires some clear space in between to be successful.

chintz

The word "Chintz" denotes the shiny glazed finish—originally wax, starch, or resin rubbed in by hand—that was applied as a dust and dirt repellent. The word is an anglicized plural of the Indian word *chint*, meaning variegated or spotted—early chintz fabrics were often printed with a small, allover motif. Indian chintzes were first imported to Europe in the seventeenth century, but it was not long before French and English textile manufacturers began developing their own, replacing the exuberant patterns of exotic birds and blooms with homely arrangements of cottage garden flowers. It is these that helped create the classic English country house style of the early twentieth century.

negate the architecture—on the contrary, it enlivens it.

Monochrome flowers

This simple glass space could so easily have looked cold and clinical, but the use of striking black-and-white floral designs has given it an exciting new dynamic. Black-and-white is the modernist's choice—but it too often makes for a stark and rather masculine interior filled with black leather, chrome, and bare white walls. Pattern is usually conspicuous by its absence, or confined to a few sterile stripes or checks. How much more dramatic—and truly contemporary —to transform a modernist room with bold black-and-white flowers! Black and white is seldom associated with flowers, though there are precedents in the intricate blackwork embroidery fashionable in sixteenth- and early-seventeenth-century Europe. Graphic and exuberant, rather than traditionally pretty, this pattern has all the impact of a Bridget Riley painting, but with an unexpected sensuosity that softens the entire room.

This is an unusual, almost eccentric use of pattern, but it is also skillful in its restraint. Too much obvious pattern, unsubtly handled, and a space such as this would end up resembling a box of licorice "allsorts" candy. The brushed linen banner at the window uses the same floral print as the wallpaper, but with the subtle addition of an ecru butterfly. Only two other patterns have been incorporated: the black flock velvet on white silk used for the Le Corbusier daybed and cushions (a witty reference to the more familiar black-and-white ponyskin original) and the simple black, chocolate, and white silk stripe at the window, which recurs once again as an edging for the cushions. The rhythm of such repetitions is what ties the look together and gives it its strong but simple style; the pattern is neither isolated nor lost in a jumble of competing prints. But look closer and you will find subtler layers of pattern beneath the surface impressions. The upholstery on the sofa might read as plain black, in order to provide the strongest contrast with the patterned wall behind, but this is no clichéd shiny black leather couch. It is, in fact, another very contemporary use of cut velvet—a rich, thick, black chenille leaf pattern on a chocolate ground; the luxury lies in the layers upon layers of texture.

Floral patterns and luxurious textures have given this room a soft sensuous quality that is certainly not associated with black and white. For all its graphic simplicity, the flower print is full of swooping curves, which echo the sleek lines of the furniture. Again, it is important to choose patterns that are compatible with the furniture and surroundings. Upholstering the daybed in velvet and silk, rather than the all-too-familiar black leather or ponyskin helps us to see it anew as the luxurious, seductive piece of furniture it is, while in this company, the curves of the Eero Saarinen table and tulip chairs are also reinterpreted in true contemporary style.

Poppies

A bold floral print, combined with streamlined contemporary furniture upholstered in modern and retro tweeds and solids, brings a daring modern touch to this ornate period room. There are no leaves, so the huge graphic blooms, in shades of pink, cranberry, and soft lilac on a crisp white satin ground, are almost geometric in their impact. The key colors of the flowers—not just the pinks and purples but the soft moss green and black-and-white of their central fringed eyes—have been picked out and repeated across a wide but subtle range of stripes, plaids, and solids. An ombré silk in mulberry shades hangs as a counter to the poppy print at one side of the window, while a woven linen stripe using the same berry, moss, and charcoal colors is used for a translucent shade. The moss green, also used in a linen cushion on the sofa and another chair, brings out the deep brilliant pinks of the poppy flowers. The moss also threads itself, with flecks of pink, turquoise, black, and white, among the yarns that make up the chenille plaids, tweeds, and retro-style weaves.

The shocking-pink check on one of the sofas and footstool has all the elegance of a Chanel suit and though clearly textured, reads as solid—vital as a breathing space when such strong, large-scale patterns are in play. The other sofa has a more complex, plaid pattern, again weaving in the moss green, while the multi-checked cushion has a subtly retro feel, complementing the chrome-legged furniture and white table.

Various blue and white porcelain and china plates and dishes from Japan and China, made between 1700 and 1900, and painted with typical patterns of flowers, figures, and animals.

Pictorial

One of the most fascinating categories of pattern is that usually referred to as "pictorial" or "conversational." Loosely speaking, this include designs that depict some real creature or object (except for flowers, which, as we have seen, have a category of their own). Animals, birds, and mythological beasts come under this umbrella, whether in the form of cute teddy bears, William Morris's famous "Strawberry Thief" design with its thrushes, or the exotic dragons, lions, and phoenixes of ancient Chinese silk. Animal-skin patterns are also included (yes—even leopard and jaguar spots and tiger and zebra stripes), along with feather, insect, and camouflage designs. Architectural, celestial, nautical, equestrian, marine, fruit, fake fabric, and anything incorporating the human figure, are just some of the many types of pictorial pattern that have been popular through the ages.

Prints in the pictorial category are often called "novelty" prints, as their appeal was often more subject to changes in taste and fashion than other, more neutral motifs—patterns commemorating a historical event, or inspired by a contemporary pastime, art movement, or film. Nautical flags and ropes, art deco airplanes, and Disney characters have all been very popular—and lucrative—in their day. Pictorial patterns may have been subject to the fickle whims of popular taste, but they are of huge and lasting interest to social and architectural historians.

Sometimes a single animal or human motif is separated from its natural environment and rhythmically repeated across the ground to form the pattern, often accompanied by geometric or floral ornamentation. At other times, a whole section of landscape—from the bridges and weeping willows of willow-pattern-inspired designs to mid-twentieth-century renditions of hunting scenes and the Wild West—becomes the motif and is repeated, in just the manner of smaller-scale spots or flowers, across the entire ground. Ultimately, it is not the exact identity of the objects chosen as motifs that makes the impact, but the patterns they create. Close up, the shepherd and his mistress on a length of brown-on-white toile de Jouy might look like a fine etching; hung as draperies and glimpsed from far off, it is the contrasting colors, complementary shapes, and interplay of forms caused by the repeat that create the lasting impression on the mind's eye. Indeed, those same components, but very differently portrayed and arranged, could be used to create hugely varying designs—simplified and printed in bright colors, and surrounded by a striped and

floral border to form a Provençal-style fabric, for instance, or pared down into a graphic 1950s screen print.

Pictorial motifs abounded very early on in the history of pattern, and similar ones crop up all over the world, either due to the mysteries of the zeitgeist or as a result of the exchange of ideas, designs, and goods along the trade and traveling routes. A pair of birds or beasts flanking a tree was a popular motif in ancient Assyrian art and found its way, probably via the Silk Route onto Byzantine silks, medieval heraldic patterns, Venetian brocades, and fifteenth-century Spanish linens. Often, the West laid a veneer of Christian symbolism over such overtly pagan devices—the Tree of Life becoming the symbol of Paradise, and so on. Many of the exotic beasts underwent a similar mutation as they passed from East to West; the fire-breathing dragons of Northern Song- and Jin-dynasty silks (900–1300 AD) had become stylized almost to comic proportions in the chinoiserie fabrics and papers that were fashionable in eighteenth-century Europe.

Peacocks' feathers and trumpet-wielding angels were popular in the nineteenth century, and designs commemorating achievements in the sciences, technology, and space travel—often in a style influenced by abstract modern art—abounded in the 1950s and 1960s. Today, after a brief interlude when geometric and floral designs held sway in the 1980s and '90s, pictorial patterns are very much back in vogue—pretty, witty, or just plain beautiful—with inspiration coming from influences as diverse as digital computer imagery, retro home magazines, and blue and white ceramics. At Designers Guild we have recently based a family of fabrics around the design of an old Sèvres teacup while the jewel-bright fruit on page 115 are a new interpretation of the Provençal look. The possibilities are endlessly inspiring.

Blue and white

From the simple stripes of Cornish ware to the familiar scenes on willow-pattern plates to the pretty sprigged patterns of calico dresses, the partnership of blue and white has a fresh domesticity about it that looks at home in a variety of interior styles. Often associated with traditional country houses, from those of colonial New England to those of Gustavian Sweden, it is also a great choice for modern rooms and has a natural association with the seaside.

When the scheme is limited to two colors, with perhaps just one contrasting accent, it is easier to be bold when mixing patterns. All shades of blue can be teamed with white or off-white, from nautical navy to invigorating turquoise to the prettier shades of powder, sky, and baby blue. Blue and white stripes, checks, and plaids are timeless classics, looking fresh and simple on their own, but given a touch of sophistication with the addition of floral prints or a geometric weave. Keep most of the patterns simple for the strongest effect, using different textures to create extra contrasts—the soft sheen of a striped silk cushion imparting a little luxury to a cotton-clad bed or the filmy freshness of voile filtering the light from an open window. Into this mix, just one more intricate pattern can be introduced with great dramatic effect—such as these plate and teacup designs inspired by Minton pattern books from the 1830s.

Blue and White China

With the earliest examples dating back to thirteenth-century China, the patterns of blue and white porcelain have lasting appeal and provide plenty of inspiration for fabric and wallpaper designs, from the gardens and landscapes of early Ming pieces to more delicate Japanese birds and flowers to the familiar eighteenth-century English Willow pattern. Early examples were dark, but by the seventeenth century Chinese potters were creating clear and brilliant blues specifically for the Dutch market. Dutch and English ceramicists followed suit, opacifying their lead glazes with tin oxide to create Delftware and tin-glazed earthenware.

Blue and white color schemes were often used in dining rooms, to coordinate with the blue and white porcelain that would be used at the table or displayed around the walls. Here, the teapots are a witty modern take on that tradition, and the china being used is an eclectic mix of vintage blue and white patterns and modern plain black and white. The room has a Scandinavian feel, with its black-and-white tiled floor, pale painted paneling, and cool, clear light. Clever use of pattern enhances this—the fresh, modern teapot print complemented by a textured printed stripe at the window and on one chair, and a woven stripe inspired by French linens (both in shades of blue and white) on the table. The furnishings are all fresh and unfussy —simple unlined curtains, a hemmed runner on the table, and a loose cotton chair cover.

Stencil

This is an ancient technique in which color is applied to cloth or paper through the open area of a cut-out motif. The bands that keep the pattern in place are fragile and dictate that the design must be "broken" in places. The Japanese first used stencils in the eighth century and still make the most sophisticated examples, with intricate designs held together by silk threads or hair, so the pattern does not have to be broken. Screen printing is a development of this technique, with the pigment forced through a fine silk gauze screen masked off to form the pattern.

Chinoiserie

In the bedroom opposite and above right, inspired by Asian ceramics, the plate design hung like a banner behind the bed mixes well with the chinoiserie-style bird and flower print used for the draperies and cushions. Eastern bedrooms often make use of fabric hangings on the walls, and, although such banners can be made in any fabric, they are particularly suited to strong pictorial designs such as the one used here.

This is a good example of how an original and abundant use of pattern can bring an air of luxury to a room of quite modest dimensions. The windows are hardly high, and yet long, billowing draperies maximize the impression of decorative pattern and luxury—a good tip for smaller rooms. Patterned and embroidered cushions pick out the blues, pinks, and reds of the principal designs, and a fine striped wallpaper lines two walls. With plenty of white on the walls and a damask bedcover, the abundance of rich pattern is never overwhelming.

In the cooler blue and green bedroom below, chinoiserie-style flowers are mixed with stripes for a more tailored and traditional feel. But note the individualistic touches: the easy chair upholstered with the floral design outside and stripes within; the carefully orchestrated mix of stripes and other patterns in the cushions on the bed, panels of the screen, and different fabrics hung at the window.

103

Modern toile

The scenic and figurative patterns of toile de Jouy are still associated with grand country houses. So it was an exciting challenge to use toile-inspired designs in the white modern apartment overleaf. The red and white toile de Jouy quilt on the arm of the sofa was the starting point, giving us a strict two-tone color scheme, and the sofa, armchair, and floor cushions were covered in solid-colored linens. For a contemporary look that complements the architecture, pattern has been confined to fine details—the cushions on the chair and ceramics on the table—rather than being used for large areas. The canvas painted with a contemporary toile-inspired landscape ties the whole look together, linking the large scale of the sleek modern furniture with the smaller handcrafted pieces. The embroidered cushions on the chair are shown to dramatic advantage against the solid red fabric; they have much more impact than if they had been piled high on a striped or flowered sofa.

Concentrating the pattern in a few carefully chosen spots in an otherwise minimalist scheme draws the eye immediately to these unique decorative elements, with their rich historical and Eastern overtones. The result is an interior that is modern and at the same time, infused with a fascinating sense of history.

Toile de Jouy

Toile originally meant simply a cotton or linen cloth, but the word has become a shorthand for large-scale, engraved scenic designs printed on fine cotton in a single color—usually red, sepia, black, or blue. The scenes were often pastoral and romantic and were copper- or roller-printed—a technique that allowed the fineness of the detail to be transferred onto cloth. The first printed toiles were Irish, but the technique was soon mastered by the French; "toile de Jouy" is often used as a generic term for all these designs, whatever their provenance.

Pictorial stripe

The way in which the pattern is used, rather than the pattern itself, is what dictates the style of a room. Here, the same teacup print, in graphic black-and-white and used in a pared-down modern way, creates a very different style and mood from the Provençal-style room on pages 118–121. The strong vertical stripes of the design have been accentuated by using the fabric as a simple blind on the window (the other blinds and wallpaper use a plain stripe alone) and as an asymmetrical runner on the sleek glass-topped table.

Although the architecture is period, the style of this loft conversion is minimalist modern, with bare white walls, a polished concrete floor and streamlined fittings. The furniture is all very modernist in style—the Verner Panton chairs in moulded black-and-white plastic, the clear Plexiglas barstools and suspended circular chair. Against this purist, monochrome backdrop, the teacup pattern stands out as a strong visual focus, and has as much impact in the room as a painting or a quirky work of art. The pattern is what gives this room its character: without it the style could easily seem cold and clinical. And to maximize its impact, it has been used extremely sparingly. The only other patterns in the room are stripes—also monochrome blacks, grays, and off-whites—used for the shades, other upholstery and cushions. Notice the way that even small details such as the stripes on the modern black-and-white china pick up on the printed fabric design.

Hand-painted wallpaper featuring a typical chinoiserie design of bamboo and birds at Château de Maintenon, France, created in 1760.

110

Chinoiserie

A French term for the European style of decoration based on Chinese motifs, which reached its peak in the eighteenth and early nineteenth centuries. Hand-painted Chinese wallpapers appeared in London in the late seventeenth century and were popularized by Madame de Pompadour in France. These exquisite concoctions, often featuring birds, plants and then-exotic flowers such as chrysanthemums and overblown peonies, inspired many imitators and were featured in many of the great English country houses.

Celadon vase

Vase patterns, usually inspired by Chinese ceramics, were used to decorate textiles as early as the end of the fourteenth century, and vases were one of the most popular motifs of the Renaissance, when classical Greek and Roman designs were woven into damasks and silks. After falling into disfavor, vases regained popularity during the reign of Louis XIV of France, when they were used to adorn an important series of figured Lyons damasks; since then, they have cropped up frequently in formal designs, often filled with flowers or fruit, or surrounded by swags of flowing drapery.

The large design used in this paneled living room is loosely based on Asian cloisonné enamelware, printed here in sepia, celadon yellow, and green on a woven damask ground. This layering of pattern on pattern adds richness to the design, which suits the sophisticated style of the room. Different patterns of wallpaper have been used in each of the main sections of the wall, with a lime green damask pattern below, while a damask patterned rug in the same brown, chartreuse, and natural colors brings the patterning onto the parquet floor. The fabric design has two different vases and more complicated flowers than the wallpaper, and is alternated at the windows by a chartreuse and sepia cut velvet. A few bright accents of scarlet and pink are vital to bring a vibrant note of contrast.

Orchard

Fruit motifs are a natural choice for rooms where eating will take place, and the orange, lemon, and cherry design, in fresh citrus and berry colors, sets a vibrant mood in this conservatory dining room. Provençal prints traditionally featured the olives and other fruits that were the livelihood of the rural southern French population, against a background of simple stripes, bright flowers, and other natural motifs. Here, the pattern is painterly rather than structured, seemingly sketched onto the fabric, with only the fruits themselves colored in—the wallpaper used on one wall is again a simplified version. Note how the exact colors of the fruit have been echoed in a simple printed stripe—a mix of patterns that nods to the Provençal style but adopts a refreshing contemporary palette.

The strong stripes are the key to keeping this look fresh and modern—too many flower and fruit prints could become cloying. Plenty of neutral colors—the off-white of the fabric, the gray stripe and outline of the fruit design, and the subtly subdued paintwork of the house—allow the fresh, fruity colors all their natural zest and prevent the combination from looking overcrowded.

As modern life grows more and more artificial, bringing flower and fruit prints into our homes is a way of keeping in touch with the cycles of nature. Here, the "modern rustic" theme is taken up by the curly cast-iron chairs and the simple painted cupboard doors.

Stripes always look good in a garden—the simple graphic patterns

are the perfect foil for nature's natural shapes and organic curves.

Provençal

Brightly colored Provençal prints get their name from Provence, in the south of France, where the patterns were used for clothes and furnishings in the early nineteenth century. Fruit and floral motifs were popular, often mixed with striped borders or with the addition of rustic figures and other pictorial subjects. The imagery was often taken from the sunbaked landscape, which makes such patterns particularly suitable for rooms like this that look onto a garden or overflow out into it during the warmer months. Here the small raspberry design printed on striped linen is the most obvious nod to French country, but it is the mix of prints and stripes, in berry reds and natural linens, that creates this charming contemporary take on Provençal style.

The pretty raspberry print is used for key items of furniture, and as a dado-height border on the neutral-striped walls. It is complemented by a clever mix of printed and woven stripes—some inspired by vintage French linens and mattress tickings—used for the remaining upholstery, draperies, and cushions. The addition of the teacup and teapot designs is a bold and unexpected move, which lifts the whole room beyond the conventionally pretty look associated with Provençal prints. Its quirkiness brings a contemporary edge to the traditional architecture and painted French furniture, the print on the wallpaper contributing another layer of pattern. The cheerful yet restrained palette is what makes such a bold mix of patterns possible. There is not even much plain white as a backdrop in this room—which makes the mix even more pronounced, like a microcosm of a Provençal fabric, with its various motifs all cleverly mixed into one. Though there are many different images and patterns in the room, they have been repeated at regular intervals, like motifs in a patterned fabric, so that the effect is not jarring to the eye.

The same stripes in fabrics treated for the outdoors bring an *en fête* feel to the garden in summer and are hung as simple shades in the conservatory to prevent it from becoming too hot.

Sèvres and Limoges

The decorative, colorful porcelain of Sèvres and Limoges in France was the inspiration for this delightful cup design. The china patterns themselves are rather grander and more formal than Delftware, and their delicate femininity is perfect for this elegant paneled French dining room. The painted cups have been printed onto classic white damask with added accents of gold, but the freehand style, using clear bright colors, gives the luxurious fabric a fresh charm and modernity. It looks especially lovely here, accessorized with a collection of fashionably mismatched vintage china and fresh garden flowers.

Another china pattern—the plate design featured on page 103—is used at the windows, with a rich cherry red border featuring fruit and flowers, which picks out one of the principal colors in the cup print. An extra drapery in red, pink, and turquoise striped silk (all colors taken from the china cup design) is hung between the two plate-patterned draperies to break up the impact of so much figurative pattern, while a woven red Provençal stripe covers the seats of the chairs. Lots of white—on the damask background fabric and on the walls and whitewashed chairs—is the secret behind this successful combination of complex pattern and stripes. As a rule, the richer the mix of patterns in a room, the greater the need for plenty of white, to prevent it from becoming too overpowering.

Nineteenth-century pattern book of silk weaves, with ribbons of contemporary Designers Guild silk designs. Pattern books were annual or seasonal records of a textile mill's production.

Geometric

The category of patterns known as "geometric" includes some of the very simplest designs, such as the pinstripe and polka dot, as well as some of the most complex, from the intricate and ingenious patterns of Moorish mosaic tiled floors to American patchwork quilts using thousands of tiny templates, to multicolored jacquard checks, in which each of many contrasting colors has to be set up by hand on a complicated loom. Geometric patterns include not only dots, stripes, checks, and plaids, but any pattern formed from shapes and motifs that are not a picture taken directly from life. Cube patterns, for instance, are geometrics until translated into a pictorial image of a child's building, and so is a basket weave until a designer makes it into a basket print. Perhaps surprisingly, the stylized fleurs-de-lis of traditional silk damasks are also classed as geometric—deemed too far removed from the natural world to be true florals. And we must not forget dots. From the linked hoops of "Double Wedding Ring" quilts to the polka dots of itsy-bitsy bikinis, the circle has long been one of the most popular of the nonfloral motifs.

The earliest patterns made by man were probably spots or stripes—simple marks and shapes that would have been scratched or daubed in repetitive sequence on the ground, or stamped with hands or rudimentary tools in a primitive precursor of the modern printing process. Prehistoric people may not actually have discovered the principles of what we now know as Euclidian geometry, but they certainly used them subconsciously—crossing stripes at a variety of different angles to form squares, checks, and diamonds and combining circles, dots, and straight lines to arrive at hexagons, stars, and other interesting, nonfigurative shapes.

Ancient motifs

Though they may look purely abstract, research suggests that the earliest seemingly geometric designs may perhaps have had pictorial intentions. The formal bands of what look to us like zigzags, stripes, and checks on a length of carved bamboo from the Malay Peninsula may, in fact, be heavily stylized representations of the sea, trees, and lightning in the sky above. Many of the characteristic geometric patterns of Guatemalan embroideries have names that indicate their origins—the "twisted snake" (figure-eight)

motif; "four-headed eagle" or "dead turkey" (a flattened bird shape with downward-pointing claws). Other geometric patterns may have been infused with symbolism long since lost to us. The circle—whether part of an ancient Indian mandala or Egyptian ceiling frieze—was a sign of oneness and eternity and of the cycles and renewal of human life and the natural world; the pyramid was a shorthand for immortality and the cube one of a number of forms known to the Ancient Greeks as "Platonic Bodies," each with a particular philosophical notion attached.

Some of the earliest motifs, later worked into repetitive patterns, may have been linked with the development of calligraphy—efforts to denote individual or tribal ownership. As writing progressed, and changes in religious and social organization took place, pattern making was free to become more decorative in intention, even if some of the original significance lingered.

Complex geometric designs

Some of the most beautiful geometric designs in history are to be found in the tiled, pierced, or painted floors, ceilings, and walls of Islamic palaces and mosques. Because of the prohibition against religious imagery in Islam, craftsmen pushed the possibilities of abstract geometric pattern to the limit. Studying such design is a fascinating first step to understanding geometric pattern and how it is formed. Whereas triangles, squares, pentagons, and hexagons can be arranged to fit together in an allover pattern with no spaces between, once the shapes have more than six sides, other shapes, such as diamonds and squares, can crop up in between, adding further to the richness of the design. When some of the most complex-looking Islamic patterns from the walls of the Alhambra Palace in

Granada, Spain, are dissected in this way, it becomes clear that they can actually be achieved using basic compass techniques, creating interlocking circles and drawing lines between them to create hexagons and stars.

For centuries now, geometric patterns have been enjoyed purely for their visual appeal, from the familiar checks and allover plaids that we see and use everyday to more elaborate herringbone tweeds and tartans in contrasting colors, and the plethora of diamond- and harlequin-based retro designs that are currently making a comeback. Geometric patterns bring a decidedly more masculine and tailored look to an interior than do feminine florals or sumptuous silk damasks. Depending on the fabric and colors used, they can be fresh (blue and white cotton), businesslike (gray-striped flannel), or elegantly refined (silk cut velvets or self-striped satin).

These patterns range from timeless classics, such as ombré silk stripes and humble mattress tickings, to the jazzy, abstracted dots and squares of the 1950s and '60s, and the modern-day takes on tartan and retro prints featured on the following pages. Geometrics are also good mixers. Teamed with other types of pattern—black-and-white stripes with rosy chintz, for instance (as on pages 78–81), plaids with stripes (as in the modern loft on pages 140–143)—there is no end to the exciting effects and moods that can be created. Despite their more disciplined appearance, geometric patterns are the group that perhaps offer most freedom for the designer—both in the creation of new patterns themselves and in the endless different ways in which they can be used.

Schiaparelli stripes

Before wallpaper was widely used, stripes were often painted directly onto walls, sometimes to imitate the effect of striped fabric in the interior of a decorative pavilion or marquee. And since wallpaper went into mass production in the nineteenth century, stripes have always been among the most popular designs. Whereas narrow stripes blur into a single shade from a distance, wide stripes keep their impact and can be used successfully in rooms of any size. Don't be afraid to employ them in small spaces—used cleverly, as here in this entrance hall, they can add drama and even make a small area appear bigger.

Textured stripes with the powdery feel of painted plaster have been used here to create a calm but strong backdrop for a few carefully chosen pieces of furniture. In two shades of pink with fuzzy blurred edges, they are as soft as the geometric style comes—accentuating, rather than competing with, the architectural console table, curved Warren Platner chair and stool, and black Carbon chair.

Schiaparelli, or hot pink, is as charming as it is unexpected and, paired with a paler shade, brings a femininity to the black-and-white tiled floor and the bold linear forms of the furniture. Three distinctly different stripes—the wide painterly pink on the walls, the fine crimson and white linen at the windows, and the lustrous multistriped cut velvet on just the backrest of the chair—have been used together with great success, the contrasting textures and dimensions linked by color.

A touch of black-and-white in the smart plaid silk cushion picks up on the scribbly lines of the Carbon chair; and the floor, while using just one nongeometric pattern—a swirling cut velvet floral—for the padded seat of the chair, brings a glamorous femininity to this stunning piece of furniture.

Textured wide pink stripes are as soft and feminine as the geometric styl

gets and provide a harmonizing backdrop for the striking linear furniture.

Modern classic

Just as vertically striped clothes can make a person appear taller, so floor-to-ceiling stripes have been used throughout history to accentuate the dimensions of formal rooms. The striped silks and velvets traditionally used in drawing rooms and dining rooms were often in somber colors— dark reds, greens, or blues, alternated, perhaps, with cream, gold, or gray. Here, however, luminous orange, pink, moss, and mimosa stripes have been used to bring new life to the second-floor drawing room of this grand Venetian palazzo. With its ornate cornicing and stunning painted ceiling, the room needed a formal treatment that honored the gravitas of the architecture, but one completely devoid of heaviness. Jewel-bright stripes are the perfect solution. The drapery fabric is woven in finest silk with a small jacquard motif worthy of Venice's history as an erstwhile capital of silk weaving, but using stunning contemporary colors. Leaving the simple valances unlined allows the sunshine to illuminate the fabric like stained glass. To break up the stripe and bring a further note of modernity, additional asymmetrical draperies have been made in a pink ombré silk stripe and a pink and moss silk damask. The mixture of patterns—continued in the rich pink and moss flock patterns on the tablecloth, cushions, and chair backs—only adds to the feeling of timeless opulence in a grand period room.

A low modern sofa, almost as long as the draperies are tall, is the dominant piece of furniture in the room and provides a balancing horizontal. Stripes have been used here, too, but with a change of fabric and texture. Though the bands of lustrous cut velvet echo the color scheme of the draperies, the distribution—and thus the impact—of the colors has been reversed. Where the overall effect of the draperies is orange, the widest stripes on the sofa are in moss green and yellow—a subtle touch and yet another method of ensuring harmony within diversity. To tie everything together, the finer pink stripes are picked up in pink silk flock-patterned bolsters, and the orange in ruffles, fringe, and other fancy trimmings.

Both the silk and velvet striped fabrics are strong enough to make an impact from a distance— vital in a room with such grand dimensions—but they also have a fineness of detail that more than stands up to close scrutiny. Using nonstriped patterns only for smaller details, such as cushions and upholstery on the carved wooden chairs, allows the different stripes to dominate but never overpower. And note the attention to detail that continues the use of stripes right through the entire scheme: even the bolster cushions have striped silk ends, and the appliqué embroidered pillows have silk insets at the sides.

Cut velvet

The technique for weaving velvet was probably invented in China before 100 BC, and would have been introduced to Italy by Persian exiles. The word derives from the old French 'veluotte', from the Latin 'villutus' meaning 'shaggy hair'—a reference to the fact that the soft pile of velvets are woven by pulling long weft loops through the warp threads. In cut or 'cisele' velvets —invented in Venice, where the opulent sheen on velvets made it popular with artists in their paintings— some of the pile loops are sheared to create intricately textured patterns. Depending on the depth of the cut, the base fabric is often visible as a contrast in color as well as texture.

Vertical space

Stripes set a smart, tailored look, which is totally appropriate in this streamlined city apartment with its minimalist detailing and shiny lacquered floor. Yet the colors used—warm crimson, cerise, and orange—bring a joyful exuberance not often associated with such spaces. Stripes stand out particularly strongly against white, and their effect has been tempered in places by judicious use of solids; one wall of the apartment has been painted bright pink, while one of the windows has simple unlined draperies in pink and crimson, which add a certain softness to that end of the room. Plain cushions in slightly textured cottons have been piled on the large striped sofa—its slightly more complex stripe in contrasting colors and varying widths needs the contrast of solids to calm it down. The matching sofa opposite has been covered in a textured pink cotton that reads as solid, although the warp threads have been space-dyed to give a subtly mottled, or "strie" effect. More solid-colored cushions, some with contrasting-colored backs, are mixed here with a fine check, using the same color palette as the draperies. Note the mattress ticking stripe on the white leather Barcelona chair and the braided cushions on a modern Perspex chair—an interesting meeting of materials, styles, and cultures. The dark sculptural shapes of lamps, vases, and other accessories have been chosen to accentuate the graphic simplicity of the stripes.

Modern graphic

Timeless classics, black-and-white checks or plaids are particularly effective in showing up the graphic high contrasts of pattern. They are also timeless classics. A bold black-and-white might seem an unconventional choice for this large modern sofa; but, in fact, the relatively small scale of the plaid and the classic nature of the pattern make it look as smart and tailored and utterly acceptable as a man in a custom-made tweed suit. Its monochrome colorway means it can be paired with a surprisingly complex pattern on the wall behind. This modern take on damask brings a lightness and almost rococo grace to the minimalist architecture. Any more than one wall would have been too much, but a fabric version of the pattern with an additional flower motif is used, along with a discreet black-and-white stripe, as informal sliding banners at the window.

On close inspection the black-and-white plaid does, in fact, have nubby "fancy yarns" running through it in contrasting turquoise and bright pink. These both soften and enrich the pattern and make it easy to choose checked, textured, and solid-colored accessories in coordinating and contrasting colors. The geometric jacquard plaid on the easy chair and stool are in a multicolor pattern, which includes the same pinks and turquoise and draws the different elements in the room together. This is a bold yet harmonious mix of patterns that works because of the limited and subtly orchestrated range of colors.

The classic nature of the black and white check allows it to mix

with the complex rococo swirls on the walls in the same colorway.

Check on check

Plaids and checks are good mixers. They encompass an astoundingly varied group of patterns, from fresh red and white gingham to glamorous silk tartans and the luxurious nubby tweed of a smart Chanel suit. In all their different incarnations, the essence of the pattern is this: that the meeting of two perpendicular stripes—whether in the same or contrasting colors or textures—produces a third element in the design which is somehow more than the sum of its parts. In many fabrics, such as the tartans and a variety of other woven plaids shown here, the crisscrossing lines can be clearly seen, creating blocks of concentrated color that stand out from the two-toned bands on either side. In others, like the bright pink tweed of the sofa, a fragmented plaid design is woven into an ostensibly solid fabric using textured "fancy yarn" (this time in turquoise), making the plaid more of a texture than a clear pattern. Plaids and checks are easier to mix than one might think. For instance, many tweed and tartan designs have become such classics that they almost read as neutrals within a lively scheme. Tartan has a timeless appeal, which has traveled far from its native Scotland. Reworking the age-old arrangements of stripes and plaids in new and unexpected colors—here a mix of lilac, pink, and bright moss green— brings a quirky contemporary charm that can work in a variety of settings, from bachelor pad to baronial castle.

Timeless quilts

Some of the liveliest geometric patterns are formed by patchwork—the technique of sewing together small pieces of different fabrics to form a larger design. A handy way of using up small scraps of cloth that are good for nothing else, patchwork was traditionally produced in the Midwest during the Depression. The *kantha* cloths of India, and, patched *Boro* overalls of Japanese cotton workers are great examples. Some of the most famous quilt patterns are American, from complex appliqué designs to the restrained minimalist squares and diamonds of the Amish communities; and their descriptive names—"Log Cabin," "Tumbling Blocks," and "Grandmother's Flower Garden"—have become as deeply engrained in the country's heritage as the heirloom quilts themselves. In the famous "friendship" and "album" quilts, many members of an extended family or community would work on individual sections of the quilt, which would then be joined together, often with some sort of geometric inlay or border to bind them, and the quilting part would often be done at all-day social events, or "bees." Women with little or no knowledge of mathematics were capable of planning and piecing the most intricate geometric designs, transforming scraps of cast-off fabric into breathtaking harmonies of color and proportion to add beauty to their surroundings and hand down through the generations. It was commonly believed that quilt designs should incorporate a deliberate fault—a mismatched color, for example, or pattern slightly askew—as a reminder that only God can make a perfect object.

Shown here are examples of the quilts of Gee's Bend, a small and remote African American community in rural Alabama, which are some of the most vibrant quilt designs in existence, a remarkable fusion of folk art and techniques with bold, abstract genius. The patterns and colorways of the quilts, often created by three or four generations of the same family, transcend the humble feed sacks and fabric remnants from which they are made and possess a heart and soul seldom associated with geometric design.

Beach house

Simple stripes and plaids in crisp cotton and linen have a fresh, breezy style that is perfect for seaside living. In this white wooden beach house, a cotton plaid, ticking stripe, and ikat design in fresh denim blues, sea greens, and naturals have been used to create a youthful, relaxed feel that is totally in keeping with the surroundings. The striped shades at the windows have all the simple charm of a beach hut awning or windbreak, filtering, rather than blocking out, the sunshine. Two simple padded chairs have been pushed together to make an impromptu sofa and upholstered in a comfortably coordinated mix of stripes, plaids, and solids—note how the plaid cushion on the striped chair is crucial in pulling the different patterns together. Two slightly more complex patterns bring an air of understated sophistication to the scheme: the blue-and-green stripe, with its black-and-white ikat detail on the low padded stool, and the funky dotted cotton used for cushions. The clear blue of the ikat stripe is repeated in the sofa cushions and woven plastic mat, while the green crops up again in another cushion made from cutouts taken from the dotted fabric. Sometimes just a single cushion can transform a room. Here, the appliqué embroidered cushion, with its plaid back and ikat-striped side panels, not only draws all the patterns in the room together in a fresh and witty way; it also introduces a welcome new accent color, dusky rose pink.

Rustic textures

The discreet striped tickings used for mattresses and upholstery in eighteenth-century Europe were the inspiration behind this striking range of woven linen stripes. They are perfect for this New England weekend cottage, with its painted tongue-and-groove walls and bare polished pale wood floorboards. A neutral, natural palette sets the tone for a modern rustic look, with comfortable, unfussy furnishings. Using two different stripes on the low, boxy sofa is a witty modern twist—a charcoal, gray, peat brown beige, white, and sand woven fabric for the framework and a contemporary mattress ticking in slate blue and coffee for the cushions. Note how the stripes have been orchestrated to run down the arms. The other furnishing fabrics are solid-colored, apart from a fine ecru and granite plaid on the low padded stool and the magnolia flower on woven damask at the window. The simplicity of this scheme is its strength.

Most stripes and plaids mix happily, provided the colors and dimensions are harmonious. In this room, keeping to a natural palette of stone and earth colors makes for an especially calm and relaxed atmosphere. Acid yellow-green is the perfect accent color—used for one billowing linen drapery, a trim on the flowered drapery, and a single silk cushion—it lights up the room like sunshine.

Ticking

Stout twilled (diagonal-weave) cotton, closely woven in colored stripes on a cream or white background, was traditionally used for covering mattresses. These days, the smart yet simple stripes are increasingly seen as a chic furnishing fabric, where its hard-wearing qualities and honest, no-nonsense design make it a popular choice for everything from upholstery to shades, curtains, and draperies. The most common ticking designs are the simplest—just one-color stripes in a regular formation on a white or neutral ground. But there are splendidly bright and complex ones to be found, often French and Scandinavian in origin and far too beautiful to be kept hidden under bed sheets on a mattress.

Tailored tweed

Bold mixtures of stripes, plaids, and geometric prints were a feature of 1950s and '60s design, and this style has made something of a comeback in recent years. The graphic patterns are the perfect complement to the sculptural shapes of modernist and contemporary furniture. In this sleek white interior, the Moorish-inspired pattern of the wallpaper, coupled with the multicolored jacquard weave on the armchairs, creates a fashionably retro feel, with patterns, shapes, and colors reminiscent of the 1950s but used in new and surprising ways. Upholstering the pair of easy chairs in an alternating mix of plaid and textured weave, with contrasting fabrics for the frame and cushions, is a clever touch, while another chair is covered in a bright pink tweed. The color scheme is cleaner and fresher than the murky browns and oranges often favored in former decades—lime green and neutrals are further enlivened by a fine thread of pink in the tartan and jacquard weaves and in the stripe on the curtain as well as the pink tweed on the chair.

Horizontal stripes are seldom used for window treatments, but the simple shade, made from a linen weave, is in keeping with the low, horizontal nature of the furniture and works in counterpoint to the vertical printed stripe on the other window banner.

155

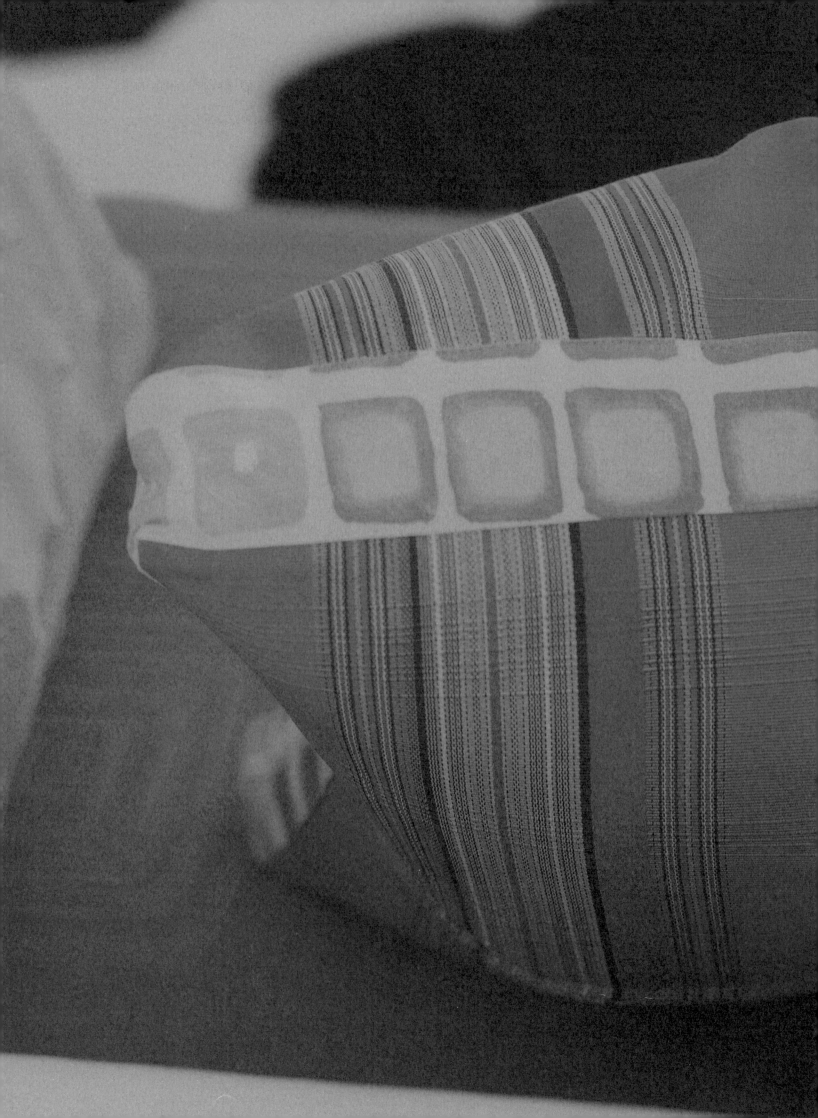

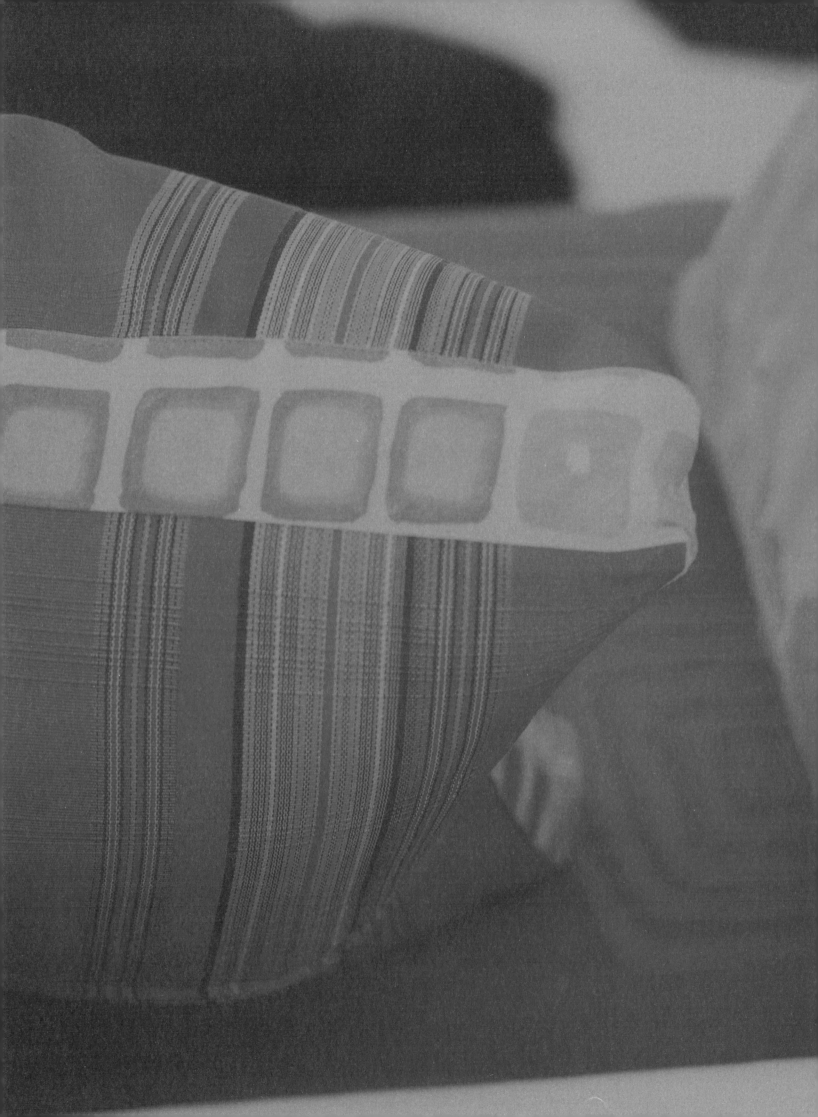

Retro

Geometric patterns in a retro-inspired style are perfect for this modern white loft. The uncompromising lines of the architecture provide a geometric backdrop, so slightly softer patterns have been used for the furnishings than standard stripes and plaids. The beautiful blurred wide stripe used on pages 132–35 has been employed here to cover the dividing wall with its integral display shelf—this time in two shades of blue. Shelves like this were often a feature of 1960s and '70s design, and the slash of white works well here, cutting across the vertical stripes in a strong horizontal. Additional retro inspiration can be found in the fabric used to upholster the interiors of the white leather sofas—a soft-cornered square-within-a-square design in reversible woven linen and chenille. These irregular geometrics again have something of the 1960s and '70s about them, and their quirky charm works well here in clear shades of turquoise and lime. The patterns used for the other soft furnishings were also chosen for their slightly retro feel: the multicolored jacquard plaid, with its op art associations, and the small pink square design used on a floor cushion, in particular. Softened lines and curves are also present in furniture and fittings: the graceful "Arc" lamp, Le Corbusier chaise longue, and swoop-backed Saarinen chairs bring sensuality to this stylish modern room, and even the triangular glass-top table Noguchi has soft, rounded corners.

Contemporary and antique silk saris and kantha embroidered scarves from Tricia Guild's own collection, built up during many years of travel throughout all parts of the Indian subcontinent.

164

Indian inspiration

India holds a very special place in the history of pattern. Any visitor to the subcontinent cannot help but be deliciously aware of the plethora of pattern that makes everyday life, though often poor and deprived by Western standards on one level, so decorative and joyous on another. From the delicate white-on-white traceries of the Taj Mahal and the kaleidoscope decorations of the Samode Palace, to the winking mirror-work embroidered costumes of Gujarati, Sindh, and Rajasthani women, to the gaily painted exteriors of bicycle rickshaws and Sikh-owned haulage trucks, to the piles of dye powder, fruit, and flower garlands lined up on roadside stalls, the Indian creative spirit finds expression in every conceivable material and situation. Pattern is not only decorative—though the silk embroidered saris and densely quilted kanthas, must rate among the most beautiful fabrics in the world—but in some cases as a shorthand form of identification. The many thousands of people who gather at the annual cattle and camel fairs in Rajasthan can tell not only the district but the village that a man comes from by a single glance at the color and pattern of his turban.

Technical skills and regional designs have been passed down from family to family over countless generations. As in many parts of the world, a large portion of a girl's youth was traditionally spent sewing a trousseau or dowry in preparation for the day when she would begin a new life as a married woman in her own home, taking her family's skills and patterns with her. Though this still happens in remote rural areas, life is changing fast, and the beautiful hangings for sale today are more likely to be the work of women who married thirty or forty years ago, with much new embroidery done for the tourist or export market, rather than for their own use. But in spite of the beginnings of commercialization, Indian textiles still retain much of their traditional charm and originality.

The development of the Indian textile industry encompasses the rich cross-fertilization of cultures that characterizes India herself: Mogul with Rajput; Muslim concepts with Hindu craftsmanship; ancient styles and techniques with British Raj tastes. Over the centuries, great centers of textile production sprang up all over India, with some especially renowned for particular patterned fabrics: Kashmir for its finely embroidered shawls, Jaipur for its decorative block-printed cottons, Varanasi for its handwoven Benares silk brocades, Kutch, in Gujarat, for its intricate embroideries, Sindh regions for their *bandhani* tie-dyes, and southern India for the gold-embellished Kanjeevaram silks, much prized as bridal saris. Nowhere can pattern be isolated from the vibrant use of color for which India is still so famous. In a country where entire cities, such as Jodhpur, can be painted a heavenly blue in

honor of the god Krishna, color is still deeply imbued with symbolism, with saffron yellow associated with religious asceticism, red with fertility, white with morning, and Day-Glo pink (dubbed by Diana Vreeland the "navy blue of India") flung about with raucous abandon at the annual spring festival of Holi.

As far back as the fifteenth century, Indian textiles were lauded across the world, with custom-made products exported to the royal families of Thailand, Burma, and China, as well as Italy, France, and Britain. So delicate were Indian printed muslins that when they were laid on the grass at dawn to dry, they could be mistaken for dew, while the finest woven shawls could be drawn through a small wedding ring.

Long before the West plundered their patterns and copied their techniques, skilled Indian craftsmen had developed highly sophisticated printing methods, including the "mordant-dye" technique, which kept cloth colorfast even in hot sun and water. Only in the 1700s were the French and English able to discover the secret for themselves; until that time huge quantities of patterned cloth were imported from India every year. And the relationship continues. As the following pages illustrate, the patterns of India are an enormous source of inspiration for Designers Guild today.

Spirit of India

Since the earliest days of Designers Guild, I have had a love affair with India and its kaleidoscope of colors and patterns. The textured blue wall of my bedroom at home in London was directly inspired by the city of Jodhpur, in Rajasthan, where the houses of the Brahmin caste are painted this extraordinary shade. It found its way into my psyche and has remained there ever since. Blues are usually cool, but this has quite a bit of red in it, while never slipping over into mauve, and is perfect for a bedroom.

Saris—in which the pattern can be woven, gold-embroidered, tie-dyed, or ikat, according to the part of India in which they are produced or the purpose for which they are worn—are an endless source of inspiration, as are the hand-embroidered kantha cloths, in which favorite fragments of antique fabric were patchworked together. The highly decorative wedding outfits— sometimes so heavily embroidered that the fabric ground can hardly be seen—are also a great fascination; the green silk embroidered with a flower design in black, white, pink, and red was inspired by a combination of different favorite pieces. Even the contemporary furniture has been chosen with the spirit of India in mind—the hand-carved wood and rope daybed and matching stool by Mauro Mori and the metal and enamel table by Ralph Levy, with their organic shapes and raw, ethnic textures.

Kantha

Kantha are fine needlework shawls from Bengal, which fuse quilting and embroidery skills, passed down the generations over thousands of years. Originally devised as a way of recycling old brocade saris and dhotis, the soft, worn cloths were layered together, smoothed on the ground, and then carefully stitched together with neat rows of running stitches right down the length. Traditional kanthas were used as quilts, floor coverings, or wrapping cloths for valuable items, while the most decorative, incorporating the most precious old fabrics, were made as gifts for weddings, births, or other family celebrations.

Tranquility

People of India have an intuitive sense of color and pattern, which is endlessly inspiring for me as a designer. The little painting on glass above my bed—picked up on travels in Rajasthan—shows an astonishing color sense and free, fluid draftsmanship. Its blues, mauve, and pinks, with the occasional accent of yellow or fresh green, were picked up and continued throughout the room and can be seen here in the variety of patterns that decorate the large white bed. The kantha quilt is a particular favorite, with its bands of contrasting floral prints, while the borders of the saris—some new, some antique—are all woven and embroidered with intricate filigree patterns.

Paisley designs are a timeless classic, which continue to inspire contemporary fabrics such as the silk stripe on the pillow; the ancient *boteh* motif can be translated into any manner of modern styles and materials but it will always be associated with India. Against the crisp white backdrop of the bed coverings, the different patterns can be admired in all their fine detail. The Indian finds look different transported from their native environment; though it is always beautiful to see them in their original context, they can be appreciated anew here in their modern, minimal surroundings. The sprinkling of mauve delphinium flowers is a modern English homage to the Indian custom of floral garlands and offerings in temples.

Burnished

A modern take on a traditional Indian block print was the starting point for this drawing room. Block prints were among the earliest designs printed in India, commonly used for everything from clothes to bedcovers. They remained popular well into the days of British rule, when they were often used in new, rather formal ways, to decorate colonial houses. This design, inspired in part by the *mendhi* patterns painted on women's hands for weddings and other occasions, is printed in gold on a heavy linen ground. Along with a burnt-orange silk in a damask design, it has been used to make unlined, unpleated draperies that allow the soft, filtered sunlight to accentuate the different patterns. The colors of Indian miniatures—burnished orange and a soft pistachio green—have been used to bring warmth to the cool neutral backdrop of putty plaster walls and pale terra-cotta floors. The harmonious mix of patterns includes an ombré silk on the square stool, a yarn-dyed tweed on the sofa, and stripes and damask weaves on the silk and velvet cushions—all in shades of the same unifying orange, green, and neutral colors.

Next door, a wallpaper inspired by block print in pale neutral shades is the perfect complement for the patterns on the antique painted furniture. The Indian-inspired use of pattern continues with the stunning flower print used at the windows, with its paisley printed background and border.

Paisley

The origin of the classic Indian *boteh* or teardrop pattern is hotly disputed. Some say its earliest incarnation was as the print formed by a closed fist on fabric or paper; others hold that it is a stylized plant form. Used in many parts of India to decorate painted and printed fabric and woven cashmere shawls, the design soon spread west. European taste favored elaborate allover patterns, in which the motif is surrounded by a profusion of flowing decorative forms. The name "Paisley" comes from the Scottish town, where mill owners began to copy Kashmiri shawls on mechanical looms that could manufacture them in a fraction of the time —even years—it would sometimes take an Indian to weave just one fine shawl.

179

Indian pattern

The patterns of India are too many to catalogue comprehensively, but certain designs and techniques have been particularly inspirational in my work with Designers Guild. Indian miniatures, particularly those of the Moghul period, have a style and grace all of their own. The colors used are often astonishingly original, and the fineness of detail with which the patterns of costumes, furnishings, and flowers are recorded is quite stunning.

Crewelwork is another great favorite. Coarse-textured, but often intricate, embroidery done in chain stitch with crewel wool on a cotton or linen ground, crewelwork is thought to have begun in India and is probably as old as sewing itself. The patterns strongly identified with the technique include stylized plant and flower formations, which may originate from India or may be the result of old English motifs being sent to India to be copied or modified. The style was popular in Jacobean England, and surviving examples show the wide range of influences, which may include medieval Flemish tapestry and European Gothic design. Early crewelwork was hand-embroidered, but modern examples may be produced by machine, with the resulting designs much more uniform but still endlessly attractive in their scrolling floral patterns.

Tie-dye, one of the simplest and oldest "dye-resist" methods, is another form of fabric patterning found all over India. The patterns are formed by gathering undyed cloth into bunches and tying it in a variety of ways prior to dyeing.

Everlasting Flower

The same block-print patterns in cool blues and greens create a totally different effect in this formal drawing room on the east side of the house, which receives lots of calm morning light. The flowers, linen block print, and lustrous silk brocades are joined at the window by another gorgeous flower image, woven in silk on a jacquard paisley background. Its overblown peonies and pom-pom dahlias, woven in limpid, dewy colors on a shimmering silvery ground, are as beautiful and exotic as anything the Indian emperors might have enjoyed, but with an unmistakably graphic modern touch.

One of the simplest methods of printing fabrics and papers with an allover pattern, woodblock printing originated in China and India more than two thousand years ago and is still in use today. It is one of the cheapest ways to produce patterned cloth quickly and efficiently, using colorfast inks and dyes—hence its use for everyday items such as bedspreads, clothes, and decoration. Patterns are carved into densely grained hardwood; the block is then coated with pigment and placed carefully on stretched cloth or paper and struck with a mallet. The process is repeated, carefully aligning the blocks each time, until all the material is covered. More complex and therefore expensive patterns can be produced by dividing different parts of the pattern between a number of blocks, with a different color used for each.

Use of the ikat technique is found from Central and Southern America to Indonesia and India via Europe and the Middle East. The clothes shown here are from Uzbekistan.

184

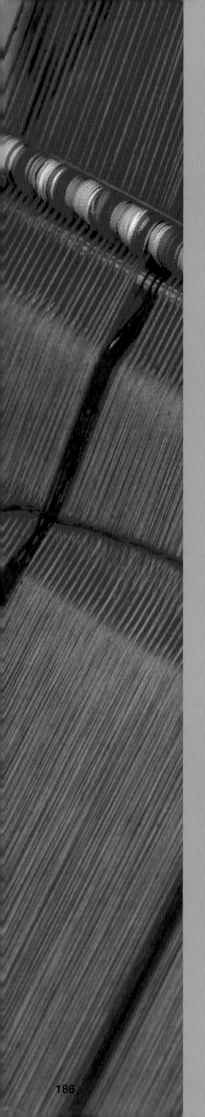

The Inca trail

Some of the most vibrant and varied patterns in the world can be found among the indigenous peoples of the Western Hemisphere to both the Native American of North America and the pre-Columbian cultures of South America. Colorful striped blankets, geometric ikat weaves, and blouses brightly embroidered with butterflies, birds, and stylized plants and animals are among some of the most familiar examples that can be found, in regionally diverse forms, from Navajo reservations to modern-day Mexico, Guatemala, Ecuador, and other parts of the New World.

Though graphic and modern in impact, many of these designs actually stretch back centuries, to ancient civilizations such as those of the Incas, Toltecs, Mayans, and Aztecs. The history of South and Central America is itself a rich tapestry of diverse cultures, with its eclectic influences woven into the patterns themselves, from the precise geometry of the pre-Hispanic cultures to the tile-embellished cathedrals of the colonial conquistadors. Spanish-imported sheep, new dyestuffs, and the European treadle loom were readily grafted onto the tradition of backstrap weaving of narrow lengths of cotton cloth for clothing, bags, and belts. In more recent times, the introduction of synthetic dyes and fibers and the impact of tourism have given yet more impetus to this exuberant mixture of Native American and Hispanic patterns, skills, and traditions.

Some of the oldest surviving fabrics in existence come from tomb excavations in Peru; but they show the characteristic stripes and zigzag patterns still common in modern-day woven rugs, blankets, and headbands throughout Central and South America. In part, these are a product of the weaving technique—straight lines are easier than curves—but evidence suggests that the zigzags were originally a symbolic depiction of lightning, while the width and color of the stripes, together with the complexity of the pattern, were often indicative of family and rank. To this day, men in the Andes still advertise their marital and social status in the patterns on their knitted hats and belts. The Guatemalan army received instruction in costume styles during the civil war, in order to identify people by the stripe sequence on their belts or ponchos and the embroidery on their shirts.

It is in Guatemala that Central America's love affair with pattern reaches its apogee. Visitors to the country, whether in a village, town, or city, are soon caught up in the bright bustle of people wearing traditional costumes decorated with birds, figures, horses, and

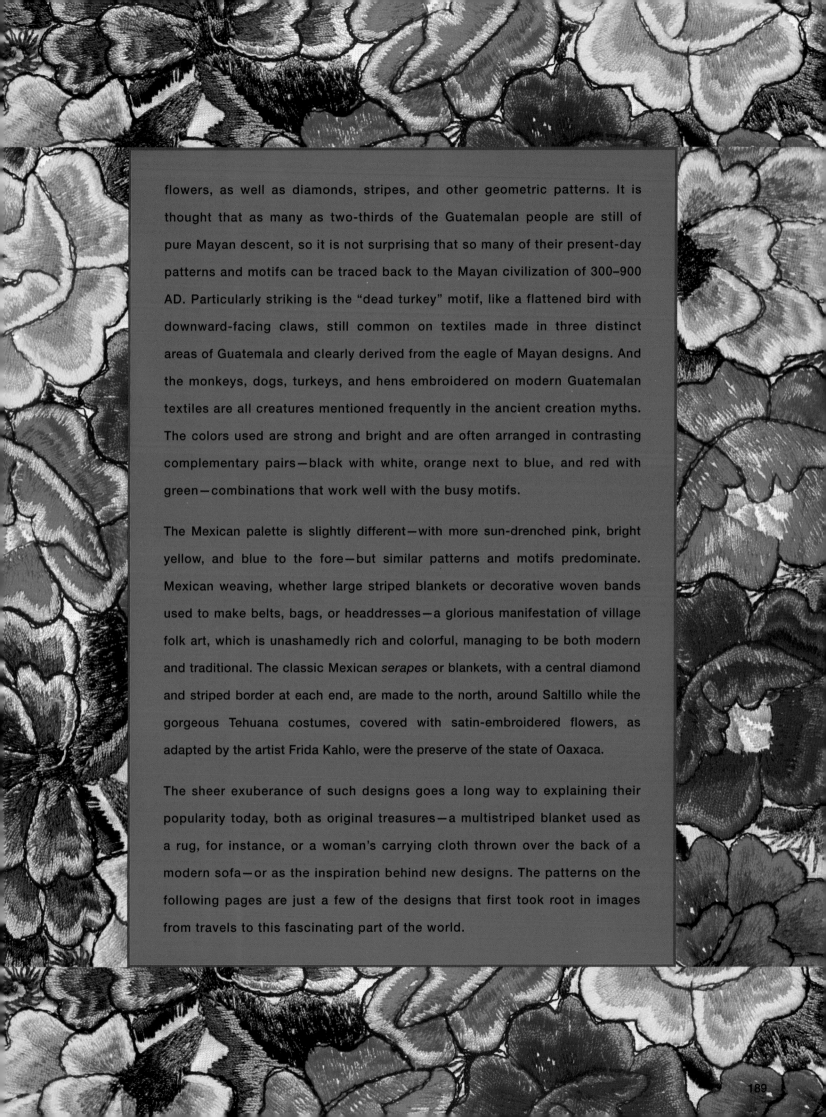

flowers, as well as diamonds, stripes, and other geometric patterns. It is thought that as many as two-thirds of the Guatemalan people are still of pure Mayan descent, so it is not surprising that so many of their present-day patterns and motifs can be traced back to the Mayan civilization of 300–900 AD. Particularly striking is the "dead turkey" motif, like a flattened bird with downward-facing claws, still common on textiles made in three distinct areas of Guatemala and clearly derived from the eagle of Mayan designs. And the monkeys, dogs, turkeys, and hens embroidered on modern Guatemalan textiles are all creatures mentioned frequently in the ancient creation myths. The colors used are strong and bright and are often arranged in contrasting complementary pairs—black with white, orange next to blue, and red with green—combinations that work well with the busy motifs.

The Mexican palette is slightly different—with more sun-drenched pink, bright yellow, and blue to the fore—but similar patterns and motifs predominate. Mexican weaving, whether large striped blankets or decorative woven bands used to make belts, bags, or headdresses—a glorious manifestation of village folk art, which is unashamedly rich and colorful, managing to be both modern and traditional. The classic Mexican *serapes* or blankets, with a central diamond and striped border at each end, are made to the north, around Saltillo while the gorgeous Tehuana costumes, covered with satin-embroidered flowers, as adapted by the artist Frida Kahlo, were the preserve of the state of Oaxaca.

The sheer exuberance of such designs goes a long way to explaining their popularity today, both as original treasures—a multistriped blanket used as a rug, for instance, or a woman's carrying cloth thrown over the back of a modern sofa—or as the inspiration behind new designs. The patterns on the following pages are just a few of the designs that first took root in images from travels to this fascinating part of the world.

Modern ethnic

Ethnic patterns and embroideries are not often associated with modern spaces—but why not? Here and on the following pages, a collection of vintage and ethnic-inspired pieces was the starting point for a vibrantly colored scheme, which brings this minimalist apartment alive. Solid colors make the perfect backdrop for patterned cushions and other treasures; and the lime of the textured wall, the turquoise slash of the sofa, and the orange of the woven rug were all taken from the colors on the ikat and appliqué patterns. These clear contemporary colors allow the intricacies of the handcrafted patterns to be shown off to best advantage.

The decorative cushions and cloths bring great joy and spirit to the room; imagine it with just the rug and sofa and see how the soul would be lost. Handmade objects have a special energy, something the painter Frida Kahlo understood well. Her embracing of traditionally embroidered clothes and headdresses spearheaded a revival in Mexican arts and crafts, and her style is still hugely inspirational today. The items here include an antique length of indigo fabric hand-embroidered with flowers, a panel of ikat-patterned embroidery, and some striped and embroidered belts, which the women used to tie up their hair. The blue and orange stripe, with its ikat detail, and the gerbera-inspired floral complement this style well; the Mauro Mori stool strikes just the right note of simple sophistication.

Coastal retreat

The ikat technique, which has been practiced in countries as far afield as central and South America, Indonesia, central Africa, and all over Asia for many centuries, is used to pre-dye the warp threads of cloth before it is woven. Derived from the Malayan word *mengikat*, meaning to bind or tie, ikat patterns are formed by tying sections of the warp threads with color-resistant twine, then immersing them in dye (often several times, in various permutations), and then weaving in the weft threads. The patterns associated with ikat are usually geometric, although the effect is often emulated in printed papers and fabrics, which sometimes bear floral or figurative designs.

In this beach house, modern ikat patterns in earthy colorways bring a touch of funky Mexican style. The orange and turquoise stripe used for the sofa and curtains has a black-and-white woven ikat detail, while the dynamic printed stripe in orange/purple and granite/blue was inspired by the fuzzy-edged shapes of woven ikats. Even the voile at the windows is decorated with delicate strips of ikat. Using only a few geometric patterns against a backdrop of lots of plain white makes the look fresh, clean, and modern—and simple cane, tin, and rusty metal furniture are perfect for this relaxed "modern country" mood.

Fresh color

A mix of patterns in a Mexican-inspired color scheme gives great vitality to this elegant room. Stripes, plaids, florals, and geometrics in lime, turquoise, and pink take the room far beyond its classical architecture and make for a truly contemporary scheme. The geometric pattern on the walls was inspired by Moorish designs at the Alhambra Palace in Spain, but the addition of flowers in the fabric version at the windows—in pink, green, and turquoise on the appliqué cushions—gives it a definite Central American spin.

This is a fine example of how different colors and combinations can transform a pattern: on pages 156–59, the same wallpaper in lime green, partnered with retro-inspired fabrics, created a totally different feel. Here, the hot pink as an accent color—in the stripe of the tartan and "fancy yarn" woven into the tweedy upholstery plaids and the embroidered cushions—is crucial in binding the scheme together and giving the room extra warmth.

The patterns used have a variety of different textures: the crispness of cotton, the softness of brushed cotton, the nubby woven plaids, and luscious cut silk velvets. Designing this room was very much like the creative process of designing a new pattern itself. Adding a bold stripe here, a two-tone floral here, a big block of plain turquoise here changes the overall balance or mood. It is a case of adding and subtracting, watching and assessing, until the desired effect is reached.

Designers Guild agents and showrooms

Designers Guild fabric, wallpaper, furniture and accessories are available from:

Designers Guild Showroom and Homestore
267-277 Kings Road
London SW3 5EN
tel 020 7351 5775
and selected retailers including:

CHICAGO

Osborne & Little, Inc.

Merchandise Mart - Suite 610

Chicago, IL 60654

Tel: 312-467-0913

Fax: 312-467-0996

CLEVELAND

Gregory Alonso Showroom

Ohio Design Center

23533 Mercantile Road - Suite 113

Beachwood, OH 44122

Tel: 216-765-1810

Fax: 216-896-9811

HONOLULU

International Design Sources, Inc.

560 N. Nimitz Hwy. – Suite 201E

Honolulu, HI 96817

Tel: 808-523-8000

Fax: 808-539-9390

HOUSTON

I.D. Collection

5120 Woodway – Suite 4001

Houston, TX 77056

Tel: 713-623-2344

Fax: 713-623-2105

ATLANTA

Grizzel & Mann

351 Peachtree Hills Avenue

Suite 120

Atlanta, GA 30305

Tel: 404-261-5932

Fax: 404-261-5958

DALLAS

I.D. Collection

1025 N. Stemmons Freeway

Suite 745

Dallas, TX 75207

Tel: 214-698-0226

Fax: 214-698-8650

LAGUNA NIGUEL

Blake House Associates, Inc.

Laguna Design Center

23811 Aliso Creek Road

Suite 171

Laguna Niguel, CA 92677-3923

Tel: 949-831-8292

Fax: 949-831-9015

BOSTON

The Martin Group, Inc.

One Design Center Place

Suite 514

Boston, MA 02210

Tel: 617-951-2526

Fax: 617-951-0044

DENVER

Shanahan Collection

Denver Design Center

595 S. Broadway - Suite 100-S

Denver, CO 80209

Tel: 303-778-7088

Fax: 303-778-7489

LENEXA

KDR Interior Resource

8510 Marshall Drive

Lenexa, KS 66214

Tel: 913-859-0400

Fax: 913-859-0483

LOS ANGELES

Osborne & Little, Inc.

Pacific Design Center

8687 Melrose Avenue – Suite B643

Los Angeles, CA 90069

Tel: 310-659-7667

Fax: 310-659-7677

MINNEAPOLIS

KDR Interior Resource

International Market Square

275 Market Street – Suite 321

Minneapolis, MN 55405

Tel: 612-332-0402

Fax: 612-332-0433

NEW YORK

Osborne & Little, Inc.

979 Third Avenue – Suite 520

New York, NY 10022

Tel: 212-751-3333

Fax: 212-752-6027

PHILADELPHIA

JW Showroom, Inc.

The Marketplace

2400 Market Street – Suite 304

Philadelphia, PA 19103

Tel: 215-561-2270

Fax: 215-561-2273

ST. LOUIS

KDR Interior Resource

10521 Baur Boulevard

St. Louis, MO 63132

Tel: 314-993-5020

Fax: 314-993-6551

SAN FRANCISCO

Osborne & Little, Inc.

101 Henry Adams Street

Suite 435

San Francisco, CA 94103

Tel: 415-255-8987

Fax: 415-255-8985

SCOTTSDALE

Dean-Warren

Arizona Design Center

7350 N. Dobson Road – Suite 135

Scottsdale, AZ 85256

Tel: 480-990-9233

Fax: 480-990-0595

SEATTLE

The Joan Lockwood Collection, Inc.

5701 6th Avenue S. - #203

Seattle, WA 98108

Tel: 206-763-1912

Fax: 206-763-3072

STAMFORD

US Headquarters/Showroom

Osborne & Little, Inc.

90 Commerce Road

Stamford, CT 06902

Tel: 203-359-1500

Fax: 203-353-0854

TORONTO

Primavera

160 Pears Avenue – Suite 110

Toronto, Ontario M5R 3P8

Canada

Tel: 416-921-3334

Fax: 416-921-3227

WASHINGTON, D.C.

Osborne & Little, Inc.

300 D Street SW – Suite 435

Washington, D.C. 20024

Tel: 202-554-8800

Fax: 202-554-8808

Designers Guild products are available worldwide.

For further information please contact:

London 3 Latimer Place
London W10 6QT
tel +44 (0)20 7893 7400
fax +44 (0)20 7893 7730
info@designersguild.com

Munich tel 01805 244 344
fax 01805 244 345

Paris tel +33 1 44 67 80 70
fax +33 1 44 67 80 71

www.designersguild.com

Author's acknowledgments

Elspeth Thompson
Meryl Lloyd
James Merrell
Anne Furniss
And to my brilliant "right hand" Jo Willer

Thank you to my team at Designers Guild for their continued support and commitment and to the following people who have participated in making this book possible:

Amanda Back, Wendy Booth, Alice Clarke, Sandii Dwyer, Liza Grimmond, Leslie Howell, Ghislaine Jamois, Simon Jeffreys, Zia Mattocks, Ciara O'Flanagan, Richard Polo, Margaret Thompson, Marissa Tuazon, Georgia Wagner

Trica Guild's Creative Manager **Jo Willer**
Project Editor **Anne Furniss**
Design **Meryl Lloyd**
Picture Research **Nadine Bazar, Sarah Airey**
Art editor **Katherine Case**
Production **Ruth Deary, Vincent Smith**
Typesetting & Artwork **redbus** 020 8996 0530

All photographs by James Merrell except the following pages: 8–9 (Russian buildings), 24–5, trace following 176, 181 left center, top right and bottom right Tricia Guild; 18–19 Linden-Museum, Stuttgart; 50–1 V & A images; 52 center right Gettyimages/Kitagawa Utamaro; 54 Heritage-images/ The British Museum; 55 below left © Photo RMN – © Droits réservés; 56–9 Natural History Museum, London; 74 center RHS, Lindley Library; 92 above Bridgeman Art Library/Private Collection, Paul Freeman; 92 above left (behind) Alamy/V & A Images; 92 center left The Art Archive/Musée Guimet Paris/Dagli Orti; 92 center right Christies' Images; 92 below Photolibrary.com/Fei Xiang/Panorama Media (Beijing) Ltd; 92–3 Bridgeman Art Library/ Private Collection, Paul Freeman; 93 above right Bridgeman Art Library/Private Collection, Paul Freeman; 93 below left Bridgeman Art Library/Private Collection, Paul Freeman; 93 below right Alamy/V & A Images; 93 below right (behind) Christie's Images; 110–11 The Art Archive/Dagli Orti; 128–9 Gee's Bend; 150–1 Gee's Bend; 170 The Art Archive/Marco Polo Gallery, Paris/Dagli Orti; 179 below left The Art Archive/Marco Polo Gallery, Paris/Dagli Orti; 179 below right Dinodia Photo Library; 180 Heritage Images/The British Museum; 181 above left The Art Archive/Victoria and Albert Museum, London/Eileen Tweedy; 181 above left Paul Harris Photography; 181 center left Hemispheres/Jean du Boirderranger; 181 below right Paul Harris Photography; 183 center right Heritage/The British Museum; 184–5 Linden-Museum, Stuttgart; 186 Gettyimages/Richard I'Anson; 187 Gettyimages/Lisl Dennis; 188 Alamy/Westend 61; 189 David Lavender.

First published in the United States of America
in 2006 by Rizzoli International Publications, Inc.
300 Park Avenue South
New York, NY 10010
www.rizzoliusa.com

Originally published in the United Kingdom in
2006 by
Quadrille Publishing Limited
Alhambra House
27–31 Charing Cross Road
London WC2H 0LS

ISBN: 978-0-8478-2892-0

Library of Congress Control Number 2006903224

Third printing, November 2007
2007 2008 2009 / 10 9 8 7 6 5 4 3

Printed in China